HE A–Z OF SOCIAL

The A–Z of Social Research Jargon

Edited by
DAVID ROBINSON
VAL REED

Ashgate

ARENA

Aldershot • Brookfield USA • Singapore • Sydney

Published by
Ashgate Publishing Limited
Gower House
Croft Road
Aldershot
Hants GU11 3HR
England

Ashgate Publishing Company
Old Post Road
Brookfield
Vermont 05036
USA

British Library Cataloguing in Publication Data
The A–Z of social research jargon
  1. Social sciences – Research – Terminology
  I. Robinson, David, 1952– II. Reed, Val
  300.7'2

Library of Congress Cataloging-in-Publication Data
The A–Z of social research jargon / edited by David Robinson, Val
Reed.
     p. cm.
  ISBN 1–85742–388–7 (pbk.)
    1. Social sciences—Terminology. 2. Social sciences—Research.
I. Robinson, David, 1952– . II. Reed, Val.
H49.5.A9 1998
300'.3—dc 21   97–49326
                                                          CIP

ISBN 1 85742 388 7

Printed in Great Britain by The Ipswich Book Company, Suffolk.

Contents

Foreword

Although there are numerous publications and locally produced handouts which set out to introduce health practitioners to research, these frequently assume working knowledge of the 'research vocabulary'. Quite often they introduce more terminology without necessarily clarifying any. Meanwhile, the growing number of research reports, theses and journal articles themselves introduce more and more terms which add to the perplexity of practitioners.

Research reports, especially those originating from unfamiliar disciplines, can alienate health carers because of their specialised presentation. Generally speaking, writers on research have only lately begun to 'translate' research terms and findings meaningfully and understandably for the practitioner.

Textbooks dealing with method frequently offer glossaries which explain specific research terms. However these are rarely exhaustive and tend to be written for the initiate rather than for the novice. Research terms need careful and painstaking presentation in order to overcome unnecessary semantic barriers. The main aim of this little book is to help break down the barriers sometimes built unintentionally by academic writers and explain key issues in accessible language.

The book, which contains more than 290 terms, is written firstly to assist those completely new to research to gain insight into the vocabulary. Secondly, we hope it will allow those already familiar with basic terms further to explore some related concepts. Thirdly, we hope it will foster creative curiosity and the desire to read further. We have taken into account issues stressed by many health practitioners; the resultant text has been carefully structured to offer the reader at all levels examples of terms and definitions in a handy format. The general 'shape' of each entry is as follows:

Term: many of these are terms used in everyday research. There are also some terms which, while not exclusive to research, are certainly relevant, since they deal with related subjects such as ethics, philosophy and informatics.

Everyday use: the colloquial or 'ordinary language' origin of a research term is given to provide the background from which it has acquired its special use. This is a short, lay explanation with meaningfulness as its first aim.

Research use: here the stipulative definition used by researchers is given. This enables the reader to compare 'ordinary language' with research versions. Equating everyday with research usage is an important step in learning research terms.

Example: here practical research example(s) are offered to help the reader establish how terminology is used. Descriptions of practical research in action have been chosen to reflect frequently occurring situations often encountered by health carers in the contexts of their daily work.

Related terms: these are listed to highlight terms usually associated with the key term. Detailed definitions of these can be found elsewhere in the text.

About the Editors and Contributors

Editors

David Robinson is Senior Nurse for Research and Development at Rampton Hospital Authority, and has been involved in full-time research since 1986. Programmes have been carried out on a wide variety of topics including: descriptive accounts of forensic psychiatric nursing care; community liaison evaluation; quality of life studies; and care and risk assessment. These have been frequently reported through conferences and publications at national and international level. Following PhD completion in 1994 he has been involved with the development of European research programmes; developing new databases in forensic research and development with the NHS Centre for Reviews and Dissemination; and is currently the chair of the National Forensic Nurses Research and Development Group.

Val Reed is a psychiatric nurse and developmental psychologist with more than 30 years' experience in research education of health professionals. He has a First Class Honours degree in education; a Master's degree in educational psychology; and a PhD in social learning studies with children with learning disabilities. He has served as scientific advisor to the Department of Health and on numerous departmental committees including the Nursing Process Evaluation Working Group chaired by Dame Phyllis Friend. His research involvement includes psychometric studies of social learning; and cross-cultural studies of health care in the United Kingdom, Egypt and the Indian sub-continent. He is currently a visiting professor in the School of Community Health and Social Studies, Anglia Polytechnic University; and research consultant to the Ashworth and Rampton Hospital Authorities.

Contributors

Mick Collins	Rampton Hospital Authority
Graham Durcan	Sainsbury Centre for Mental Health
Tom Mason	Liverpool University
Dave Mercer	Ashworth Hospital Authority
Val Reed	Anglia Polytechnic University
David Robinson	Rampton Hospital Authority

Acknowledgements

The editors gratefully acknowledge

the huge and perplexing task successfully completed by the contributors in preparing the materials for this book ('de-mystifying' research is no easy task!);

the key facilitative role of **Frank Powell**, Special Hospitals Service Authority, without whose enthusiastic support we would be precisely nowhere;

formative and highly enjoyable discussions of early drafts with members of the SHSA Nursing Research and Development Group when we met at Ashworth, Broadmoor, Carstairs and Rampton Hospitals;

the critically important work of **Bridget Bower** (Rampton Hospital Authority) and **Anne Dean** (Sheffield Hallam University) in preparing draft typescripts and reading and constructively criticising the editors' work.

Abstract

Everyday use: summary of a larger piece of work.
Research use: a two- to three-hundred-word summary giving the reader an overview of the research paper or thesis to follow. Also sometimes referred to as a *synopsis* (literally 'seeing together') or as a *summary*.
Example: seen at the beginning of theses, dissertations, articles and research papers.

Acknowledgement

Everyday use: an acknowledgement recognises the assistance received from others in bringing a task to a successful conclusion. To acknowledge someone is to greet him or her in a friendly and respectful manner.
Research use: in an acknowledgement a researcher lists those individuals or institutions who were involved in the research study. The acknowledgement is used by a researcher when writing up the research study to make sure that the contribution of every individual or resource provider who has assisted with the research is duly recognised.
Example: at the beginning of a research report in a section entitled 'acknowledgements' you may see some such passage as: 'The researcher wishes to acknowledge the help of the following ...'.

Action research

Everyday use: self-reflective enquiry undertaken by participants in social situations.

Research use: change strategy designed and implemented by those involved in describing and attempting to solve a specific organisational problem.

Example: the nursing team may use action research to evaluate an aspect of care delivery, making appropriate changes as the need for these is identified.

Related terms: practitioner research; theory–practice gap.

Analysis/analyse

Everyday use: breaking a problem down into its constituent parts for purposes of explanation.

Research use: examination of data for trends, comparisons, relationships and themes. Enables the researcher to concentrate large amounts of information into manageable form.

Example: the strength and frequency with which an individual displays a particular behaviour can be represented in a block graph.

Related terms: investigate; quantitative/qualitative analysis; statistical/content analysis.

Anonymity

Everyday use: the state of being unidentified.

Research use: the procedures taken to ensure that participants in a research study cannot be identified when the work is written up. A researcher may be collecting confidential information from participants and will wish to ensure that information cannot be linked to any individual.

Example: participants in a study may be given a code number or the opportunity to complete a research questionnaire without including any personal details.

Related term: confidentiality.

Anthropological study

Everyday use: a study undertaken in a branch of science concerned with the study of the origins of man, but also with the development of human relationships, social behaviour and beliefs.

Research use: a researcher may use an anthropological approach as a broad theoretical basis for a study. Every research study has a theoretical base; and anthropological theory may be the approach of choice.

Example: a nurse researcher may wish to examine in detail the belief systems underlying approaches to nursing care in differing cultures.
Related terms: ethnography; phenomenology.

Applicability

Everyday use: capable of being applied.
Research use: the degree to which findings of a research study are likely to have a practical use when applied to the whole population rather than just to the sample.
Example: if in a research study an intervention was found to be useful with a particular group, then that particular intervention could be *applied* to increased numbers of others with the same problem.
Related term: generalisability.

Applied research

Everyday use: research conducted to solve an everyday problem or question.
Research use: studies designed to apply research findings into practice, rather than carried out purely to increase knowledge.
Example: a study applying the theory of group interaction to designing a better social-care environment for residents.
Related terms: action research; controlled trial.

Archival research

Everyday use: use of historical records as a source of information.
Research use: collection of data from secondary sources, either in the form of books or papers, or from records or notes. Enables the researcher to prepare the ground for later empirical work or more extensive library studies.
Example: in a study of medical procedures used during the last century, no first-hand data are available and the only resources are contemporary records.
Related terms: literature search/review; meta-study; secondary source.

Assumption

Everyday use: a statement which is taken for granted.
Research use: one purpose of scientific research is to test such assumptions, to see whether they stand up to rigorous analysis.
Example: research-based care may be *assumed* to be good practice. But this can lead to complacency, and continual questioning of such assumptions is required.
Related terms: hypothesis; theory; validity.

Attitude

Everyday use: an attitude is a relatively consistent tendency to respond in a particular manner to specific incentive.
Research use: attitude measurement is a very important part of qualitative research, when a researcher wishes to find out how people feel about certain phenomena.
Example: a researcher may design a questionnaire to measure people's attitudes towards the length of time they have to wait before being seen in a doctor's surgery.

Attribute

Everyday use: a characteristic or trait.
Research use: a researcher may wish to record the attributes or characteristics of a particular phenomenon.
Example: as part of an attitude-measurement study the researcher records the following sample attributes: age; gender; occupation; income.
Related term: variable.

Average   *see* **Mean**

Axes

Everyday use: an axis is the pivotal point which determines the outcome.
Research use: the term is used to denote the horizontal (*X-axis*) and the vertical (*Y-axis*) of a line or bar graph. These are typically used to plot two variables in relation to each other.
Example: during observational data collection, data is collected about human interactions; from the analysis of results the

researcher uses a bar chart to identify the frequency of various activities. He/she employs positions on the horizontal X-axis to identify various activities and plots their relative frequencies on the vertical Y-axis.

Related terms: bar chart; histogram; line graph.

~B~

Back-up

Everyday use: a term used to describe a spare copy of a piece of work kept in case the original is damaged.
Research use: backups are essential in many research studies where large volumes of data are collected.
Example: large amounts of data which have been collected over many years can be held on one computer disc that may be easily damaged. A spare (back-up) disc is therefore essential.
Related term: back-ups are characteristically kept on *floppy discs*, which are free-standing electronic storage devices normally operated from the A> drive of a personal computer.

Bar chart

Everyday use: a pictorial representation of data.
Research use: a statistical graph in which frequency distribution is shown by equal-base rectangles above a baseline (the *X axis*) with differences reflected in the vertical height of each bar. Alternatively, data may be presented as a *histogram*, with bars of proportional width and height.
Example: the researcher may wish to demonstrate in graphic form the number of alcohol-related incidents associated with specific problems (see below):

Baseline

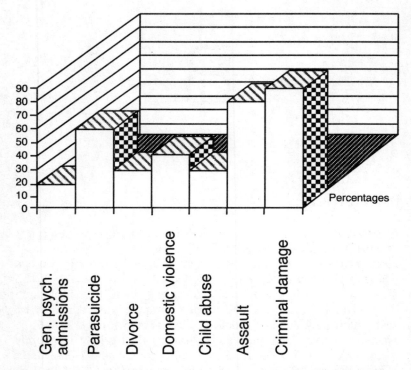

Source: Scottish Health Education Coordinating Committee (1985): *Health Education in the Prevention of Alcohol-Related Problems*, Edinburgh: SHECC

Figure 1   Bar chart showing percentage of alcohol-related incidents in a number of selected problems (after Scottish Health Education Coordinating Committee, 1985)

Baseline

Everyday use: the point from which a process starts.
Research use: a measure used to determine the state of affairs at the start of a study, before any change has occurred. The baseline provides important data against which later measurements are evaluated.
Example: following initial measurement of the frequency of breakdowns occurring by a particular make and model of car (BASELINE), further measures can be taken following appropriate action to reduce the frequency of such breakdowns.

8

Related terms: average/mean; before-after design; norm; re-measure.

Basic research

Everyday use: research undertaken to describe the nature of the world we live in.

Research use: research designed to extend the knowledge base of a discipline or profession. It enables the discipline to refine its current beliefs and modify existing thinking. This type of research is carried out primarily for descriptive purposes, rather than for the sake of its potential applications in modifying existing practice.

Example: research into the frequency and types of interaction occurring between residents and care staff.

Related terms: hypothesis; theory.

Baud rate

Everyday use: baud rate refers to the speed at which a *modem* can transfer or receive information.

Research use: data may be transferred from one computer to another anywhere in the world, provided that the baud rates of the sending and receiving computers are compatible.

Example: data collected in a collaborative study at the University of Amsterdam is sent to another computer in England at high speed. A hundred-page document may take just a few minutes to send. This will vary in relation to the baud rate (speed of transmission).

Related term: modem.

Before-after design

Everyday use: this describes a method of data collection whereby a measurement is taken both *before* and *after* the introduction of the variable under study.

Research use: this design is used to ascertain whether or not the variable under study has changed, or has had any effect on other variable(s).

Example: A researcher wishes to know if the introduction of a secretary reduces the amount of time managers spend on paperwork. The amount of time spent on paperwork by managers

both *before* and *after* the secretary's arrival will be measured. It will then become apparent if there has been any change.
Related terms: comparison; measurement.

Bell curve   *see* **Normal distribution**

Bias

Everyday use: any distorting influence.
Research use: any variable or opinion tending to distort or unduly influence the results of an investigation. Factors militating against a balanced and objective view.
Example: numerical results may be unconsciously misinterpreted as being due to a factor which the researcher is convinced plays a significant part, even though other, equally cogent, explanations are possible. Or a research design may be biased: for example, when asking nurses about care planning, only registered nurses were included in the sample. This automatically biased the sample by excluding the opinions of other nurses.
Related terms: biased sample; representative; validity.

Biased sample

Everyday use: anything *biased* is weighted or loaded in a particular direction.
Research use: a sample which is unsuitable for purposes of an investigation because its members are not truly representative of the main group under study.
Example: a researcher inadvertently includes too many mature students (that is, students aged 25 or over) in a study of entrants into university, when in fact the main group he/she is studying are aged between 18 and 22.
Related term: sample.

Calibration

Everyday use: the marking of a scale into units so that measurements can be made.

Research use: the precision of calibrations on a scale, and the level of measurement used, will determine how accurate it is. High accuracy is often required in some research studies where differences in measurement may be very slight.

Example: a researcher measuring the birth weight of small animals (for example, rats) would require a scale with finer calibrations than a researcher measuring the birth weight of human infants.

Related terms: interval scale; measurement; ordinal scale; ratio scale.

Case study

Everyday use: a study concentrating on a single or few cases only.

Research use: an in-depth investigation into a person, group, organisation or other social unit, carried out in order to understand issues that are important to the development, history or care of an individual.

Example: in order to find out how mental hospitals 'work', a group of psychologists get themselves admitted as patients. They then carefully observe and record precise details of their various wards and care routines.

Related terms: in-depth study; participant observation.

Category

Everyday use: a term used to describe a group that has similarities.

Research use: a researcher may pre-determine categories of possible answers within a particular study. Alternatively he/she may let them emerge from the data by interrogating them for possible groupings or similarities.

Example: a researcher designs a questionnaire to which each question has four possible answers – very happy, happy, unhappy, very unhappy. These may be regarded as categories: for example, 10 of the 20 people in the study responded in the category of 'unhappy'.

Related terms: analysis; data; sample.

Causal relationship

Everyday use: a relationship is causal if one event or phenomenon is caused by another.

Research use: this indicates a relationship between two variables, whereby the presence of the *cause* (variable 1) determines the status of the *effect* (variable 2).

Example: a researcher has identified an *effect*, for example lung cancer; and will carry out experimental studies to determine the *cause(s)*, one of which may be smoking.

Related terms: experiment(al); variable.

CD-ROM

Everyday use: this stands for *compact disc read-only memory*. This refers to a piece of software which can hold large amounts of data. It may also refer to the unit in which the compact disc is inserted.

Research use: one compact disc can hold large quantities of data to which a researcher can gain easy access. Such data would normally take up considerable amounts of paper or other storage.

Example: a researcher may wish to examine any references to a particular nursing intervention, and would select a database stored on CD-ROM to search for previous work.

Related terms: database; software.

Central tendency

Everyday use: clustering about a central point.
Research use: a statistical term for the degree to which scores in a distribution tend to cluster about the mean score. Central tendency is measured statistically using the mean, variance and standard deviation of the distribution.
Example: a lecturer wishes to know how his/her students' scores relate to similar scores for all students undertaking a particular test. He/she compares their scores with those for the whole group by examining the relative means and standard deviations for the two groups.
Related terms: mean; standard deviation; variance.

Chance/chance alone   *see **Significance/p-value***

Change strategy

Everyday use: any method to bring about change.
Research use: research methods used to alter practices in an organisation or discipline: for example, action research. Change strategies rely on involvement of members of the target group(s); and are characteristically used to introduce or implement research findings into practice.
Example: an action research study identifies changes needed in the delivery of care. These are implemented through a planned training and education programme to alter current care practices.
Related term: action research.

Checklist

Everyday use: to make certain something is correct.
Research use: a research checklist may take the form of a list of tasks to be carried out or as part of data collection, where the researcher scores, ticks or tallies something.
Example: in a study observing time and motion (tasks and their frequency) of engineers assembling a car engine the researcher has a checklist of assembly routines which are ticked or checked off as they happen.
Related terms: schedule; tally.

Chi-square

Everyday use: a statistical formula which compares observed with expected frequencies.

Research use: chi-squared is a non-parametric statistical test which is used to determine statistical significance between two or more sets of data. Its general formula is $[(O-E)]2/E$ where $O =$ observed frequency in a given cell and $E =$ expected frequency for that cell.

Example: in a study of planned nurse-patient interaction to facilitate self-medication, the researcher may use chi-squared to examine the difference in observed frequency of compliance between the control and the experimental group.

Related terms: control group; experiment; parametric; significance.

Classification

Everyday use: the way in which information is organised into units of similarity.

Research use: a researcher wishes to measure a phenomenon according to a particular classification.

Example: a researcher wishes to measure temperatures of the human body during various stages of physical exercise according to the classification of the Fahrenheit scale.

Related term: category.

Closed question

Everyday use: a question permitting only a limited number of answers.

Research use: a question within a questionnaire or interview schedule which restricts the answer to defined topic(s). Such questions stop the informant from digressing from the subject matter.

Example: in a study of people travelling abroad, a researcher might ask: 'Have you ever been abroad before?' (YES or NO).

Related terms: forced-choice; multiple choice; ranking; rating.

Cluster analysis

Everyday use: examines the pattern produced by scores

'clustering' together.

Research use: a process used to display data in groups. Used in observational or questioning studies in which the researcher examines specific groups in relation to a particular population.

Example: in a study of student nurses' ability to solve problems, cluster analysis may be used in relation to the variables assessment; care planning; implementation; evaluation; age group; and gender.

Related terms: sampling frame; variable; variance.

Communication

Everyday use: the exchange of information, usually by oral or written means.

Research use: a researcher studying communication within a specific social group will collect examples of communicative behaviour to investigate a particular phenomenon.

Example: a researcher wishes to know people's opinions on crime. He/she interviews a number of informants. What the informants tell the researcher will be an example of oral communication. Alternatively he/she may ask people to complete questionnaires. In this case the written answers will be examples of indirect verbal communication.

Related terms: interview; questionnaire; respondent.

Comparison

Everyday use: a search for similarities between sets of collected information.

Research use: a researcher will compare collected sets of information to find similarities which will be of benefit when presenting the information.

Example: a researcher compares completed questionnaires to establish how many respondents answered yes to a particular question.

Related terms: questionnaire; respondent.

Conceptual framework

Everyday use: a set of ideas used for purposes of explanation.

Research use: a structure which controls or displays the basic design of a research study. Ideas are assembled because of their relevance to the successful carrying-out of the study.

Confidentiality

Example: a researcher uses a conceptual framework based on theory related to communication to investigate verbal interactions between a telephonist and their customers.
Related terms: hypothesis; model; theory.

Confidentiality

Everyday use: respecting the confidence of others by refusing to divulge privileged information.
Research use: the required practice of keeping data in confidence during a research study. A token of this is the pledge given by the researcher that the research information will not reveal the identity of the people involved. Used in all research designs where the data collected are confidential. Usually a prerequisite insisted upon by ethics committees before permission is given for the study to proceed.
Example: in a study of job satisfaction, factory managers were asked to comment upon issues concerning their immediate line managers. It was essential that these comments should not be attributable to individuals.
Related terms: Data Protection Act; ethical approval; ethics.

Confounding variable

Everyday use: to *confound* someone is to *confuse* him or her.
Research use: refers to a variable affecting the results of a study which has not been accounted for by the researcher. Such variable may confuse or invalidate the findings of a study.
Example: a researcher investigating the supposed effects of stress on skilled performance omits to control for *practice effects* produced by varying ward experience in his sample.
Related term: variable.

Consent   *see Informed consent*

Consistency

Everyday use: used to refer to *regularity* and *dependability* in the behaviour of individuals and/or phenomena.
Research use: the degree of similarity of information collected on the same phenomenon at the same time by two independent observers.
Example: two observers collect data on shopping activities

using an identical data sheet and procedure for timing of observations and rest periods between active observational sequences.

Related term: inter-rater reliability.

Construct

Everyday use: specific phenomena or theoretical notions are identified as *constructs* for purposes of scientific investigation.

Research use: a researcher may be interested in investigating elements of psychiatric nursing, and will develop various constructs or theoretical components to produce as comprehensive a model as possible.

Example: a researcher observes that a substantial proportion of psychiatric nursing activities appears to involve nurses and patients socially talking to each other. Subsequently this type of activity may be codified as 'patient-social' (that is, staff–patient interactions involving social content). This then becomes a *construct* within the ambience of the total study.

Related terms: model; theory.

Content analysis

Everyday use: a detailed consideration of the contents of anything.

Research use: the reviewing of verbal data to elicit recurrent themes. The systematic and objective procedure for converting written or oral communications into qualitative and/or quantitative data for subsequent analysis.

Example: in a study of attitudes to personal hygiene, the researcher examines the interview data for themes and trends picking out similarities within the findings.

Related terms: data set; theme.

Content validity

Everyday use: this refers to instruments used in a study and their ability to measure the content of the subject under investigation.

Research use: researchers subject their instruments to content validity checks to ensure that the specific items within them competently cover the area of investigation.

Example: a researcher has developed an instrument to measure

children's knowledge of road safety. He/she submits the instrument to experts in the field to establish that the questions cover all appropriate and necessary topics.
Related term: validity.

Contribution

Everyday use: something helpful which is given or donated.
Research use: the extent to which a completed research study has added to a body of knowledge. A researcher will usually include a section in a final report to describe how the work has contributed to knowledge.
Example: the results of a research study into patient aggression in prisons indicate a new intervention which, when further studied, could contribute to new knowledge about aggressive behaviour.

Control group

Everyday use: a group acting as a yardstick against which to measure changes.
Research use: in an experiment the experimental group receives the 'treatment', while the control group receives either nothing or a placebo. Used within experimental designs to test a given hypothesis.
Example: in a study to test the effects of a specific drug, one group is given the drug and the other (control) group is given a similar but inactive alternative substance. The groups are then monitored and results compared.
Related terms: comparison; experiment; hypothesis; variable.

Controlled trial

Everyday use: a *controlled* event is one which is set up and organised in a systematic and appropriate way.
Research use: a controlled trial is an experimental study carried out under strict criteria which are intended to prevent the study becoming confounded by extraneous variables or events. The types of controls applied in a controlled trial include (for example) randomisation of treatments; matching or balancing of demographic variables such as age and gender; the order in which treatments are administered; and the knowledge of the purpose and method of the study possessed by its participants.

Example: the classical example here is that of a controlled drug trial, in which the relative effects of administering varying dosages of an antidepressant drug are assessed against the progress of controls (that is, patients treated differently) who receive placebo substances or nothing at all.
Related term: control group.

Correlation

Everyday use: a relationship between people or things.
Research use: the relationship between two or more sets of data. A test to determine the degree of this relationship, and whether or not it is statistically significant.
Example: in a study of the reliability of doctor–patient interaction measures, the researcher compares previous behaviour samples with newly collected samples to determine the degree of relationship (correlation) existing between the two data sets.
Related terms: correlation coefficient/test; reliability.

Correlation coefficient/test

Everyday use: correlation (*co-relation*) implies the existence of a degree of **relationship** between two or more sets of figures. This relationship may be either positive or negative.
Research use: a formula used to show evidence of agreement or disagreement between two or more sets of numerical results. Correlational techniques are used to assess the levels of agreement existing between two or more sets of scores or other numerical data. These techniques are widely used to determine the validity and reliability of a set of results.
Example: if two researchers collecting data at the same time agree on 50 per cent of the results, this would be expressed as a reliability coefficient of 0.50.
Related terms: reliability; validity.

Corruption

Everyday use: implies adulteration or lack of purity.
Research use: refers to a situation in which numerical or other data has become confused or spoiled, usually as a result of electronic faults in data storage.
Example: due to an electrical 'surge' during data storage, three data fields have become 'mixed up', leading to the formation of a

single *corrupt* data set.
Related term:　data set.

Critical analysis

Everyday use:　to apply careful attention or judgement to something.
Research use:　during data analysis a researcher attempts to be critical of the methods he/she uses; and to keep his/her personal judgement out of the analysis of data. This process is intended to ensure that data analysis remains objective.
Example:　when recording observations of nurses' interactions with depressed patients, the researcher may have personal views on how this should be done; but he/she will attempt to keep these personal views out of the analysis, merely reporting what he/she has seen.
Related terms:　critique; objectivity.

Critique

Everyday use:　a critical appraisal.
Research use:　a systematic appraisal or critical review of a piece of research. Frequently used in a literature review to help determine the validity of previous related studies and their relevance to the work in hand.
Example:　in critiquing an article on characteristics of schizophrenia observed in a given group of patients, the researcher analyses the study's descriptive thoroughness against a model of the observational process.
Related terms:　reliability; validity.

Cross-tabulation

Everyday use:　producing tables of related figures.
Research use:　an examination of the frequency and/or magnitude of a variable in relation to analogous readings for two or more other variables. Cross-tabulation is used to establish the occurrence and degree of relationship of connected variables.
Example:　a researcher may use cross-tabulated data to examine the relationship between gender and consumption of alcohol (that is, differential consumption rates of men and women).
Related term:　frequency.

Cross-validation

Everyday use: checking the correctness of something from a number of different perspectives.

Research use: a useful method of cross-validation is to compare the results of a specific study with those of other studies of the same or similar phenomena, which have used identical or similar methods. Within a given study, a similar cross-validation can be achieved by collecting relevant research data using a number of different methods, and/or employing different data collectors. The purpose of these methods is to enhance the *validity* of the data.

Example: a researcher collecting data on the treatment of gravitational ulcers uses two different but related scales to collect data. He/she then compares the results of the two. Alternatively, data collected by two independent researchers using the same instrument(s) may be directly compared.

Related term: validity.

Culture

Everyday use: the term used to describe the beliefs, morals and lifeways of groups of people within a particular society.

Research use: such cultural groups may be studied with regard to specific cultural beliefs and practices; for example, those relating to child-rearing or to the treatment of mental illness.

Example: a researcher may identify beliefs and ideas that are specific to nurses working within forensic psychiatry, and which thus mark them out as a nursing sub-culture.

Related terms: phenomenology; qualitative method.

Data

Everyday use: the Latin word means 'things given'.
Research use: the information gathered in a study. The researcher gathers appropriate data to help describe or explain specific phenomena.
Example: in a study of client satisfaction, the verbal comments collected representing their views are the data.
Related terms: observation; qualitative method; quantitative; questionnaire.

Database

Everyday use: a piece of computer software that holds large amounts of information.
Research use: a database can be used to store or retrieve information to make it more manageable and accessible.
Example: a researcher has collected a large number of questionnaires from which he/she wishes to make differing comparisons. All the responses are entered into a database, which can then be asked to perform a variety of operations and comparisons to assist analysis.
Related terms: analysis; data; software.

Data collection sheet

Everyday use: a list or schedule for collecting information.
Research use: a paper instrument designed to facilitate collection of relevant data.
Example: a researcher studying the number and types of social interactions occurring on a public transport system designs a data

collection sheet to help him/her in collecting these data swiftly and economically.
Related terms: frequency; interview schedule.

Data Protection Act

Everyday use: refers to the Data Protection Act, 1984, and is a set of guidelines for the electronic storage of confidential information.
Research use: protects the privacy of the individual with legislation to safeguard personal information held on computer.
Example: a researcher collecting personal information about respondents (e.g. name and medical history) and entering this into an electronic database will have to comply with the provisions of the Act (which is *not*, however, concerned with data not stored electronically).
Related term: database.

Data set

Everyday use: information which has something in common.
Research use: a collection of data that have similarities. Used to organise research data into categories for ease of presentation and description.
Example: after interviewing 100 people on their views about meal choices in a canteen, the researcher finds that 20 of them have expressed a desire for vegetarian choices. The vegetarian respondents may then be allocated to a separate data set.
Related terms: data; database.

Debriefing

Everyday use: an explanation taking place after the event.
Research use: a *post hoc* session in which the researcher gives those involved in the study further details regarding its results. Usually carried out at the end of a research programme in order to inform the people involved about the study's details.
Example: in a survey to assess staff knowledge of a new procedure to prevent self-harm, the researcher first administers a questionnaire to assess baseline knowledge. Where educational deficits are identified, he may wish to feed this back to informants so that appropriate educational and training programmes can be designed and implemented.
Related terms: baseline; informant; sample.

Degrees of freedom

Everyday use: the term implies the presence of a certain amount of 'room for manoeuvre'.

Research use: a statistical term relating to a given sample or distribution of scores. It is based on the notion that, given a sample with a mean score of fixed size, all the scores in that sample are free to vary to some extent, *except for one*. This is the score left when all the others have varied; since, if the mean is to remain unaltered, this last score *must* take on a given value. The notion is largely speculative (theory); but it is of great importance as a factor determining the significance applicable within inferential statistical tests. The degrees of freedom typically associated with 'uncomplicated' samples are typically given by (d.f. = $N - 1$) or (d.f. = $N - 2$).

Example: a researcher has carried out a correlation test comparing two sets of data. Knowing that the associated degrees of freedom (d.f.) are given by $(df_1 + df_2) = (1 + 1) = 2$, he/she is able to check the levels of the test for the appropriate d.f. size.

Related term: significance.

Delphi technique

Everyday use: the Delphic oracle was renowned in the ancient world for its cryptic utterances, which frequently stimulated a variety of interpretations in its hearers.

Research use: a process in which a questionnaire is given several times to those involved; with a series of short statements summarising results at each stage to stimulate thinking. Frequently used in educational and training programmes where a degree of organisational change is required.

Example: in a survey examining knowledge of a specific technique, a questionnaire is given to establish the baseline knowledge. Following appropriate educational approaches and amendment of the questionnaire, it is given again and effects of the change in knowledge monitored.

Related terms: change strategy; reflective technique.

Dependent variable

Everyday use: something which depends on something else.

Research use: this is the central phenomenon under study in an experimental design. It is known as the dependent variable because any change(s) it displays during the study are assumed to be attributable to other variable(s) which are manipulated freely (independently) by the researcher (independent variables).

Example: in a study assessing the frequency of occurrence of lung cancer in smokers (dependent variable), the researcher attempts to measure the impact of various causal factors (independent variables).

Related terms: experiment; independent variable.

Description

Everyday use: to outline the details of a particular person, situation or event.

Research use: a researcher will describe the results of a study using both quantitative and verbal techniques.

Example: after investigating peoples' opinions on capital punishment, the researcher will discuss the varying opinions of the sample, using a mixture of verbal and description techniques.

Related term: analysis.

Descriptive Research

Everyday use: an attempt to study and describe something.

Research use: a study in which data are collected to describe and define the phenomena concerned. A qualitative research approach used to describe complex phenomena in situations where the use of numbers alone (quantitative analysis) is inadequate.

Example: in a study to investigate health behaviour in a different culture, the researcher may use participant observation and detailed notes to describe its key characteristics.

Related terms: anthropological study; ethnography; qualitative method.

Descriptive statistics

Everyday use: the use of numbers to describe the characteristics of anything.

Research use: in research statistics may be either *descriptive* or *inferential* in nature. *Descriptive* statistics refer to the collective characteristics of populations, sample or groups – for example the mean, the median, the mode, standard deviation, variance and so forth.

Example: in describing the voting preferences of a given

community, a psephologist (those studying elections) uses the arithmetical mean to help compare voting preferences of various age groups of voters in the community.
Related terms: inferential statistics; mean.

Design *see **Research design***

Determinism, deterministic

Everyday use: a 'determined' individual is one who is driven to pursue a particular course of action.
Research use: determinism is a scientific theory which states that all possible events or states of affairs in the universe are brought about by physical or biological causes which 'push' individuals to behave in specific ways. By contrast, *humanistic* scientists assign a greater role to freewill in the way that people deal with themselves and the world.
Example: a classical deterministic theory is Darwin's theory of natural selection, which states that successful species are selected for survival due to their superior capacities to survive in a more or less hostile environment.

Dichotomous response

Everyday use: dichotomous means 'cut in two' – that is, capable of taking one of two values.
Research use: in terms of questionnaire design, a dichotomous question would be one in which the respondent is given the opportunity to answer either yes or no – no other responses are allowed.
Example: in a job satisfaction study, managers were asked the following: 'Are you satisfied with your line manager? [Please tick YES or NO]'
Related term: forced-choice.

Direct (primary) data

Everyday use: information received 'from the horse's mouth'.
Research use: a method by which information is gained from respondents at first hand.
Example: a researcher interviews informants in the course of a study; and audiotapes their responses. These recordings constitute

direct data.
Related term: secondary data.

Discourse analysis

Everyday use: discourse refers to talk or interactive discussion.
Research use: the analysis of verbal data obtained during discussion or interviews. Verbal data are examined to determine their common elements or derive appropriate differential categories for use in the analysis.
Example: after carrying out a number of interviews, a researcher may carry out discourse analysis on the content to determine the exact detail of what was said.
Related terms: category; classification.

Dispersion

Everyday use: people or things are said to be 'dispersed' when they spread out from a central point or leave the scene altogether.
Research use: dispersion is a descriptive statistical term used to characterise the degree to which scores in a specific distribution are *dispersed* from the mean score for that sample. Dispersion is typically described in terms of the **mean** itself; the **range** of scores in the distribution; and the **standard** or **average deviation** from the mean observed in the distribution.
Example: in assessing the achievement levels of her students, a lecturer examines the variation among their scores in terms of the mean score itself, and the average or standard deviation for the group, in the subject she is concerned about (for variation see variance).
Related terms: mean; range; standard deviation.

Dissemination/disseminate

Everyday use: spreading the word.
Research use: research without dissemination is considered to be incomplete. Findings need to be reported to other researchers and to the wider audience it attempts to influence.
Example: a researcher on completion of a study examining attitudes of factory workers on production line management disseminates the work by publishing an article in the *Journal of*

Factory Management or by presenting the work at a seminar or conference.
Related terms: abstract; journal.

Distribution

Everyday use: a placing or scattering of people or things.
Research use: the arrangement of scores or values in a given set of data. Construction of such frequency distributions is usually the first step in organising data, since it helps by setting it out in an orderly manner to facilitate further analysis and interpretation.
Example: in almost any study, drawing a scattergram or tabulating data in a grouped or collective way enables the researcher to present data in a graphic and interesting way.
Related terms: central tendency; dispersion; mean; median; mode; scatter; standard deviation.

DOS

Everyday use: DOS stands for 'disk operating system'.
Research use: the disk operating system currently used by personal computers. It varies, but is quite frequently a Microsoft system (MS-DOS). DOS assists with running software which a researcher may wish to use within particular studies: e.g. databases; spreadsheets and statistical and graphics packages.
Example: the researcher can display data by using a DOS-based graphics package, which will display the data in pictorial form, for example as a bar chart or pie chart.
Related terms: database; hardware; software; spreadsheet.

Double-blind trial

Everyday use: the nearest is the old proverb about the blind leading the blind!
Research use: an experimental approach in which neither informants nor researchers are aware of who is in the experimental or control groups. Used to ensure that informants do not react or change their behaviour due to expectations rather than to objective effects of the independent variable.
Example: if an experiment to assess the effects of a new medication is to be conducted, it is essential that neither nurses nor patients are aware of their precise status regarding experimental and control groups, since both may unconsciously

alter their behaviour accordingly.
Related terms: control group; experimental group; trial.

~ E ~

Empirical

Everyday use: empirical events are happenings or states in the real world which can be observed scientifically.

Research use: verifiable methods of obtaining data and facts which can be measured or observed. Used in research programmes when the researcher examines what is happening in the real world through observation or questioning, rather than relying solely on theory.

Example: in a study of residents' activities in a particular care facility, the researcher may observe in order to describe and explain specific behaviours in relation to the environment supporting them.

Related terms: observation; qualitative method; quantitative; questionnaire.

Epistemology

Everyday use: epistemology is a branch of philosophy which deals with the nature of human knowledge and the processes by which we acquire our knowledge, both of ourselves and of the external world.

Research use: all research is theoretically based; and all theories deal to some extent with what constitutes valid knowledge in connection with the topic under study, and how best to acquire it.

Example: faced with the problem of removing behaviour in a client with learning disabilities which is getting in the way of effective social learning (e.g. attentional difficulties; hyperactivity), a behavioural psychologist will approach the problem by carefully examining his/her client's *reinforcement history* for clues as to what environmental events may be supporting or rewarding this behaviour. This is because the epistemic theory underlying behavioural analysis places great stress upon the importance of environmental factors in maintaining and changing our behaviour.

Error

Everyday use: the extent to which a measurement deviates from the true measurement due to inaccuracy.
Research use: researchers need to be aware of the presence of error when taking measurements or presenting results.
Example: a researcher given the task of developing blood pressure norms in a given population must adhere to a standard protocol in taking such readings. If he/she does not do so then potentially confounding variables such as the patient's position during the reading, recent exercise or level of anxiety may result in some degree of error.
Related term: quantitative.

Ethical approval

Everyday use: obtaining permission for a specific activity.
Research use: in order for a research study to proceed, it is normally necessary for ethical approval to be sought from, and given by, an appropriately constituted ethical committee.
Example: a researcher will submit a research proposal to such a committee in order to gain permission to carry out the study. This may be obtained either from a local ethics committee or in some cases through managerial approval, the latter typically in cases where patients or clients are not directly involved in the study, which is non-invasive and deals specifically with managerial issues.
Related terms: consent; ethics.

Ethics

Everyday use: that branch of philosophy which deals with the good in human affairs.
Research use: a branch of philosophy concerned with what is good or bad for research participants; and what the moral obligations of the researcher are. Ethical issues are taken into account within planned research programmes to ensure that the

rights of research participants are safeguarded. This is usually carried out by specially appointed ethics committees who attempt to ensure that these conditions are being met.

Example: in a study where the behaviour of a patient is potentially changed – for example through changes in medication or as a result of physical treatment – the researcher must ensure that strict controls and safeguards exist to protect the patient's health status.

Related terms: confidentiality; informed consent; right of refusal.

Ethnography

Everyday use: a method of qualitative research that focuses on a group of people with the aim of understanding their world view.

Research use: when little is known about a group or sub-group, this method seeks to obtain a global understanding of the views, values and beliefs of that society.

Example: a researcher wishes to understand the world-view of a specific group of teenagers who hang around street corners in gangs. He attempts to gain this understanding by living with and 'hanging out' with them.

Related terms: ethography; ethology; qualitative method.

Ethnomethodology *see Qualitative method*

Ethography/ethology

Everyday use: the ethos of a group or society is composed of those features of its ideas, behaviours and beliefs which are characteristic and unmistakable – its habitual way of life.

Research use: *ethographic* or *ethological* studies seek to study organisms or human beings 'in their natural habitat', ideally without interference of any kind. This approach is associated with the work of the Dutch ethologist Niko Tinbergen, who brought the method to bear in studying both animals and humans.

Example: Tinbergen's own studies of autistic behaviour in children relied on close observation of the child's relation to his/her environment, in an attempt to isolate precursors of autistic behaviours. The approach originated in biological studies: but when applied to humans it has many affinities with the behavioural approach, though careful to avoid issues related to intervention.

Evaluation

Everyday use: to assess or determine the *value* of anything.
Research use: the process of examining research methods and results as to their appropriateness in terms of a study's original aims. A global term that describes the critical examination of research products.
Example: a researcher wishes to carry out a study into customer satisfaction in electrical retailers. He/she carries out a literature review and finds 200 articles concerning customer satisfaction. He/she must then evaluate how many of these articles will be useful to him/her in the study: for example, some articles may relate to customer relations by telephone and will not be entirely appropriate for his/her purposes.
Related term: literature review.

Evidence-based care

Everyday use: care or practice that is based on sound evidence.
Research use: as an ideal, all kinds of care given should be based on sound evidence informed by research studies.
Example: after searching the literature regarding care of patients with pressure sores, a nurse discovers research evidence regarding particular nursing interventions that have apparently produced an improvement. The nurse adopts these interventions, basing her care on previous evidence.

Existentialism

Everyday use: anything *existential* is concerned with, or pertains to, the business of everyday life in the real world. *Existentialism* is the name given to a philosophy of existence pioneered by such distinguished modern European philosophers as Husserl, Heidegger and Sartre.
Research use: the basic notion underlying existentialism is that the world is ethically 'meaningless' – empty of values save for those which we bring to it ourselves as human beings. Therefore it becomes pressingly important that we each achieve self-actualisation – that is, make conscious, individual choices in the light of as full a knowledge as possible – if we are to live authentic lives. This leads in turn to an existential *epistemology* individual human values and needs are central data when studying

anything to do with human individuals and/or their social or corporate lives.

Example: the work of Carl Rogers on 'encounter groups' sees the group as helping the individual to achieve authentic existence by valuing him/her as a person without any attached conditions. Research based on encounter groups looks for improvements in self-worth, societal adjustment and personal relationships arising out of the therapy and describable mainly in qualitative clinical terms.

Related term: phenomenology.

Experiment/experimental

Everyday use: a method of finding out about the real world by setting up trial situations.

Research use: the classical scientific method – a process by which data are gathered in rigorously controlled circumstances to test possible causal relationships between two or more variables. Used in quantitative scientific programmes where hard data are gathered to support or disprove a given hypothesis.

Example: in a study examining the effects of a new influenza vaccine, an experimental design is used in which one group of patients (the experimental group) receive the vaccine; while the other group (the control group) receive an inert placebo injection.

Related terms: causal relationship; control group; dependent variable; hard data; hypothesis; independent variable.

External validity

Everyday use: for a thing to be *valid* it must obviously be suitable for the task in hand.

Research use: the extent to which the results of a research study can be applied to the wider population. Used to examine the generalisability of results from a relatively small sample to the wider population involved. Successful external validation serves to give local results more credibility in the wider care context.

Example: the results of a research study show that a sample of patients suffering from depression respond very well to a new drug. These results could then be applied to increasingly larger samples of patients who suffer from depression.

Related terms: generalisability, validity.

~ F ~

Face validity

Everyday use: something which appears valid or appropriate 'on the face of it' (that is, at first sight).
Research use: face validity refers to the fact that a research instrument may immediately *appear* to be valid, in terms of a rapid initial survey of its content. Face validity is used by researchers in the initial stages of research instrument design.
Example: an instrument has been developed to examine people's views on capital punishment. The instrument is given to other experienced social researchers, who are asked: 'On the face of it, in your opinion will this instrument measure what it is intended to measure?' (Views on capital punishment.)
Related term: validity.

Factorial design

Everyday use: in everyday terms, a *factor* is some feature of the situation which must be taken into account when describing or attempting to alter a situation.
Research use: a factorial design is a statistical approach to the analysis of complex factors involved in, for example, health care. Basically, the study is designed so that each 'factor' can be measured; and then the factorial measurements manipulated to reveal how much of the **variance** in scores is attributable to each factor concerned; how much is due to *interaction* occurring between main factors; and how much is *residual* – that is, not accounted for by either of these.
Example: the effects of a psychoactive drug are investigated using a factorial design involving two main factors (drug or placebo) in sub-samples matched for gender and age. Following

data collection, the patients' scores on a related instrument are compared using a factor-analysis which shows: (1) how much variation is attributable to *main* effects (i.e. drug; placebo); (2) how much variation is attributable to *interaction* effects (i.e. drug and gender; drug and age; placebo and gender; placebo and age); (3) how much variation is *residual* (i.e. unaccounted for by any of these).
Related term: variance.

Field notes/observations

Everyday use: notes or observations made during action (originally a military term).
Research use: notes or observational data collected by the researcher in the field (that is, in the real world setting). These are recorded for later analysis when the researcher returns from the field: for example, to the research office.
Example: a researcher observing the social behaviour of primates in their natural habitat (*the field*) makes notes on their behaviours (*field notes*) which he/she will later analyse.

Field study

Everyday use: a study carried out 'in the field'; that is, practically based and close to the real world.
Research use: research conducted in a real-world setting rather than in a laboratory. A field study would be carried out in a situation where the researcher needs to rule out possible confounding variables by studying the phenomenon in its natural or local setting.
Example: while studying maternal take-up of an oral rehydration programme for infants in India, workers were able to observe the incidence of infant diarrhoea and the folk methods by which this was treated. Such field-based studies using direct observation are sometimes rather misleadingly called 'field experiments'.
Related terms: anthropological study; ethnography; field notes/observations.

Findings

Everyday use: to learn or discover something.
Research use: the collection of research data, the pooling of

this and its analysis leads to the discovery of new information or information confirming what is already known.

Example: in a study observing frequency of town centre alcohol consumption in the street, the researcher found that in 65 per cent of cases it was males aged 20–22 while in the case of females the age was 18–21.

Related term: disseminate.

Floppy disk

Everyday use: a magnetic device used for storing electronic data for subsequent handling in a computer.

Research use: floppy disks are frequently used in research to store typing, spreadsheets, databases and their products.

Example: the researcher may use the computer's floppy disk drive as an alternative to the computer's internal (hard) disk to store and process various components of his/her research: e.g. data, graphs, research proposals, thesis, research papers. Often the floppy disk is used as a backup device to store extra copies of critical documents in case of damage or corruption occurring in the hard disk (internal computer storage disk).

Related terms: corruption; database; graphics; hardware; software; spreadsheet; thesis.

Fluctuation

Everyday use: the movement or 'flow' of something which is being measured.

Research use: movement in any direction of the value of a variable over a period of time; or of the sample size under study.

Example: the recorded temperature at 1800 hours every day in June, 1996, *fluctuated* between [x] and [y].

Related terms: range; variance.

Focus group

Everyday use: the term implies a group of people or things on which attention is focused.

Research use: a group of individuals who are selected (or focused upon) usually in the later stages of a qualitative study, because they are regarded as possessing experiences or views which are particularly relevant to the purpose or outcomes of the study.

Focused interview

Example: as the result of a preliminary interview, it is apparent that caregivers whose spouses are disabled find the nature and availability of respite care to be a particular focus of stress or dissatisfaction. Following preliminary analysis, the research team invite those carers who have experience of respite care (a percentage of the total sample initially interviewed) to meet and participate in an audiotaped discussion of contentious issues concerning respite care in particular. This is thus a 'focus group' in two senses: first it focuses upon an important sub-category of care, identified as such during initial interviews; and secondly, it focuses upon those individuals who are perhaps specially able to contribute in view of their own experiences as carers.

Focused interview

Everyday use: to *focus* upon anything is to make it an object of special interest.
Research use: an interview schedule constructed to concentrate questions around a specific topic of special interest in terms of the research programme.
Example: such a schedule could be used to stimulate discussion in the type of focus group discussed above.
Related term: interview.

Forced-choice item   *see* **Dichotomous response**

Frequency

Everyday use: the number of times an event occurs.
Research use: again, the number of times an event or phenomenon occurs. Frequency is used as a numerical index mainly within quantitative research programmes.
Example: in a study of religious practices within an ethnic community, the researcher may wish to count the number of times (i.e. the frequency) with which cult members attend religious gatherings.
Related term: quantitative.

Frequency distribution

Everyday use: an ordered display of values.
Research use: enables data to be examined systematically.
Example: the results of an examination in marks out of 10 for

ten students were as follows: 2, 2, 3, 4, 6, 6, 9, 9, 10. The frequency distribution would be: lowest score 2; highest score 10 (giving a *range* of 8). Two occurred three times; 3 occurred once; 4 occurred once; 6 occurred twice; 9 occurred twice; and 10 occurred once.

Related terms: range; variance.

~G~

Generalisability/generalisation

Everyday use: general applicability.
Research use: the degree to which findings may be expected to apply beyond the specific situation in which they occurred. The case for applying such findings in more general situations.
Example: success of a particular drug in controlling the symptoms of depression in a specific sample may lead to more widespread use of the drug with all types of depression.
Related term: representative.

'Goodness of fit'

Everyday use: this is a commonplace term which has acquired a special statistical meaning. In common-sense terms, it indicates that two or more items are specially suited or fitted to each other (for instance, we speak of 'fitting like a glove').
Research use: a test for 'goodness of fit' is a statistical test which is designed or adapted to demonstrate how close the distribution of scores in a specific sample comes to a theoretical distribution; for example, the normal curve. This is particularly important when deciding which statistical tests should be used on the data. If the 'goodness of fit' test shows that the distribution is reasonably close to the normal curve (see *normal distribution*), then *parametric* tests may be used. If however, the distribution is skewed or departs appreciably from normality, then tests are limited to suitable *non-parametric* alternatives.
Example: before running a comparative test on a sample of data ($N = 100$), a researcher wishes to know if the data are sufficiently normally distributed to justify using a parametric statistical test. She therefore passes the data through the chi-

squared test for 'goodness of fit' to a normal distribution. In this case the data prove to be appreciably skewed: therefore she knows that she would be better advised to use the non-parametric equivalent of the t-test (in this case the Wilcoxon matched-pairs signed-ranks test).

Related terms: normal distribution; skewness.

Graph

Everyday use: a pictorial way of illustrating results.
Research use: a way of illustrating data in pictorial form.
Example: the number of YES/NO responses to a question may be illustrated by means of a bar chart.
Related terms: bar chart; distribution; histogram; scattergram; X–Y axes.

Graphics

Everyday use: this term is nowadays usually applied to computer-generated illustrative materials such as 'clipart'; screen savers; and video games.
Research use: refers to specialised graphic utilities and software which can be used to generate figures, tables and illustrative diagrams for inclusion in research papers and reports.
Example: for administrative purposes, a factory manager uses a numerical graphics pack to generate a table of sickness absences occurring among staff during the preceding twelve months.
Related term: software.

Grounded theory

Everyday use: a theory grounded in reality.
Research use: an approach to collecting data with the aim of developing theory based on real-world observations. An inductive approach which uses a systematic set of procedures to generate theory about social processes. Used to construct theory where none exists or where current theory is inadequate. The approach is closely associated with the names of its originators, Glaser and Strauss.
Example: the approach may be used in clinical, management or educational contexts where little is known: e.g. characteristics of patient relations in an accident and emergency ward.
Related terms: inductive theory; observation; phenomenology; qualitative.

Halo effect

Everyday use: an impression produced by an individual's 'halo': that is, his/her personality and characteristics.

Research use: halo effects surrounding individuals can lead to false assumptions regarding their likely abilities or behaviour. This would have the possible effect of biasing research results.

Example: a researcher observing levels of achievement in trainee social workers may rate certain individuals consistently higher than others because they have become more friendly towards him/her than the others.

Related terms: bias; Hawthorne effect; subjectivity.

'Hard data'

Everyday use: 'hard' carries with it the connotation of tough and dependable.

Research use: a colloquial way of referring to the data typical of the natural sciences (for example physics, chemistry, biology) which are generally to do with fixed, invariant properties (length, mass, time) and reach sophisticated ratio measurement. Quite often the term is used in discussion to differentiate these data from the 'soft data' typically generated in the social sciences.

Examples: these include (e.g.) brain weight in grammes; rate of saltatory conduction in nerve-muscle preparations; galvanic skin responses; corneal reflex latency in milliseconds.

Related term: 'soft data'.

Hardware

Everyday use: durable components made largely of metal and plastic.

Research use: the electronic equipment which makes up a computer (e.g. video display unit; base unit (central processing unit, CPU); disk drives; keyboard; modem; cables).

Example: questionnaire responses (*data*) may be inputted into a database (*software*) via the computer keyboard and disk drives (*hardware*).

Related terms: central processing unit (CPU); keyboard; software.

Hawthorne effect

Everyday use: an effect which is due to people being aware that they have become the focus of attention.

Research use: the effect on participants in a research study caused by the fact that they know they are under observation. An effect produced by altered environment which may be confused with an experimental effect. The name comes from the Hawthorne Works in America, where the effect was first noted.

Example: a researcher notes that frequency of factory workers increases whenever he/she is present and seen to be observing the work routines.

Related terms: confounding variable; dependent variable; halo effect; independent variable.

Heterogeneity

Everyday use: the state of being different.

Research use: when an attribute is extremely varied in a group under study, the group is said to be heterogeneous with respect to that attribute.

Example: the attribute of height in a group of eighteen-year-olds is relatively heterogeneous when compared with height in a group of two-year-olds (whose height will be more similar).

Related terms: attribute; homogeneity; variable.

Histogram   *see **Bar chart***

Historical research

Everyday use: studying details about past events.
Research use: the collection and evaluation of data relating to past events which may lead to a clearer understanding of past or present events.
Example: a researcher may wish to examine the stages by which a particular treatment was introduced into a care context. By examining minutes of meetings and other records, and by interviewing staff who were there for the whole period, he/she would gain a clearer picture of its introduction.
Related terms: archival research; retrospective data.

Homogeneity

Everyday use: the state of being similar.
Research use: the degree to which people or things under study are similar. An attribute which is very similar within a group under study is referred to as a homogeneous variable.
Example: height in a group of two-year-old children is a relatively homogeneous variable.
Related term: heterogeneity.

Hypothesis

Everyday use: a hunch or educated guess as to why something occurs.
Research use: statement of a predicted outcome which the research will either support or disprove. An initial prediction or statement of expected results which is tested through research. Two types of hypothesis are commonly used in experimental research. The *null hypothesis* predicts that the independent variable(s) manipulated by the researcher will have no effect on the dependent variable. Conversely, the ***experimental** hypothesis* predicts that the independent variable(s) will exert a significant effect on the dependent variable.
Example: a researcher hypothesises that students who have failed a particular examination, and who subsequently receive individual tuition before re-taking it, will have a better chance of success than those who receive no individual tuition.
Related terms: dependent variable; independent variable.

Hypothetico-deductive reasoning

Everyday use: working out causes and possible solutions on the basis of a 'hunch', intelligent guess or more developed theory.

Research use: the process of reasoning from global concepts to something specific. A researcher produces a hypothesis from the examination of a particular theory.

Example: a researcher has examined educational theory and found that students who receive individualised tuition have a better exam success rate. From this he/she deduces (or hypothesises) that nursing students preparing for final examination will have a higher success rate if given individualised tuition.

Related term: hypothesis.

Independent variable

Everyday use: something which can be varied at will.
Research use: the factor(s) or variable(s) in an experimental design which are under the control of the researcher. Such factors are manipulated to test their causal relationship with the phenomenon under study (the dependent variable).
Example: in a study to assess the causal relationship between smoking and lung cancer, the independent variable is the act of smoking. Here the researcher examines rates of occurrence of lung cancer in various groups of smokers and non-smokers, to assess the degree of relationship which exists.
Related terms: causal relationship; dependent variable.

In-depth study

Everyday use: anything done 'in-depth' is pursued with a considerable amount of rigour and application.
Research use: refers to studies in which data are collected with care using relatively sophisticated methods; and then subjected to strict analysis.
Example: experiences of parents with their autistic child are studied in-depth by following-up initial interviews with a series of focus-group discussions; and by videotaped interaction sequences which are subsequently analysed frame-by-frame.

Inductive theory

Everyday use: the word means 'to take in', i.e. to observe.
Research use: development of inductive theory involves a

process of inductive reasoning: that is, the arrival at a general conclusion from a particular set of observations.

Example: a researcher may observe that patients who are treated with electro-convulsive therapy (ECT) experience brief disorientation after each treatment. From this he/she may generalise that disorientation is regularly associated with the use of ECT.

Related terms: empirical; generalisation; hypothetico-deductive reasoning; theory.

Inferential statistics

Everyday use: statistics used to help infer the reasons underlying a particular phenomenon.

Research use: statistical tests (statistics) which allow the researcher to make generalisations based upon findings from a sample. Because a researcher is rarely able to sample a whole population, inferential statistics allow generalisations to be made about the population from the sample itself.

Example: the use of correlational techniques to assess the degree of relationship existing between (e.g.) pattern of professional training and attitudes to care and treatment.

Related terms: descriptive statistics; generalisation; population; sample.

Informant *see* **Respondent**

Information systems

Everyday use: denotes a variety of methods for conveying information, ranging from more traditional forms such as journals and newspapers through to computer databases and electronic networks.

Research use: information systems offer specialised services to researchers, including electronic searches; 'search engines' (that is, vehicles for obtaining data via the Internet); mail bases and noticeboards; and home pages which may be dedicated to a specific research project.

Example: as part of her induction, a research student learns how to access CD-ROM and online databases (e.g. CINAHL, MEDLINE), and how to obtain information relating to health care research on the Internet through (for example) Infoseek (CINAHL and MEDLINE are health information databases).

Related terms: CD-ROM; database; literature review.

Informed consent

Everyday use: a situation in which someone agrees to take part in a research programme after being told the details of the study.
Research use: people who are to be involved in a research study need to be able to make a decision to participate based on the premise that they fully understand all its implications and procedures.
Example: potential participants in a research study are provided with a full summary of the project to which they are being asked to contribute. They are usually asked to sign a consent form to indicate their willingness to participate.
Related terms: ethics; participant.

Instrument

Everyday use: a piece of apparatus used to perform a delicate or intricate task.
Research use: a device or technique employed by the researcher to collect and record data. A global term used to describe the various data collection techniques used.
Example: examples include interview schedules; questionnaires; checklists; and data collection sheets.
Related terms: data collection sheet; interview schedule; observation schedule; questionnaire.

Interpretation

Everyday use: to show the meaning of something.
Research use: when setting out to answer research questions or prove/disprove hypotheses the researcher when analysing the data seeks to understand the meaning of his findings. This is carried out by comparing what is known to what has been found and translating this into the written word.
Example: a researcher collects data in its raw form, he/she carries out analysis to make it meaningful and interprets this using the written word or graphs/tables.

Inter-rater reliability

Everyday use: the level of agreement between two or more raters.
Research use: the consistency shown by data collected on the

same phenomenon at the same time by two or more independent raters.

Example: in a study of nursing activities, two observers watch a nurse undertaking a specific series of activities, and make detailed notes on their observations. Results are then compared to confirm the degree of similarity. The closer the results, the more accurate or reliable they will be.

Related terms: consistency; observation; reliability; validity.

Interval scale

Everyday use: information that is scaled in equal units.

Research use: an interval scale is a precise measurement scale in which equal distances on the scale represent precisely equal amounts of the characteristic being measured, but without including a zero point.

Example: a clinical thermometer measures body temperature precisely for a given range: e.g. 95–110 degrees Fahrenheit.

Related terms: . nominal scale; ordinal scale; ratio scale.

Intervention

Everyday use: a strategy used to change events.

Research use: a manipulation introduced by the researcher in order to test a specific hypothesis. Often used within experimental design and action research programmes.

Example: where preliminary research has shown a lack of necessary knowledge or skills on the part of staff, an educational package (intervention) may be introduced and monitored to assess its impact over time on knowledge and skill levels.

Related terms: action research; experiment; hypothesis.

Interview

Everyday use: a face-to-face discussion typically involving two people.

Research use: a method of data collection in which one person asks questions of another. Used to elicit precise information from participants to throw light on the research hypothesis.

Example: in a study of a new consumer production, the researcher asks the respondent what, in his/her opinion, are the advantages of it compared to others.

Related terms: respondent; semi-structured interview;

structured interview; unstructured interview.

Interview schedule   *see* **Schedule**

Investigate   *see* **Analysis**

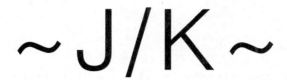

~ J / K ~

Jargon

Everyday use: language which is hard to understand because it is full of special words, or apparently ordinary words used in a special way.

Research use: strictly speaking, there is no place for mere jargon in any area! However, within any discourse which deals with abstract concepts or specialised subjects, there will be a component of related terms which, if not understood, will be seen as 'jargon'. The complexity of health care research, with its numerous philosophical approaches and related methods, means that many people are unfamiliar with much of its terminology. Quite often single phrases classified as 'jargon' in fact refer to a complex of related issues; and are essential if the complex is to be fully understood.

Example: for those just beginning research, there will be an early phase when almost all research terms will seem to be 'jargon' – hence the need for this book!

Related terms: conceptual framework; protocol.

Journal

Everyday use: a personal record of situations or events.

Research use: a regular publication featuring research articles and theoretical papers. A researcher will use thematic journals at differing levels of complexity for dissemination of research findings at local, national and international levels.

Example: in a study of mental health issues relating to nurse education, the researcher may publish in an appropriately thematic journal, such as *Nurse Education Today*, to ensure

dissemination to a targeted audience interested in the topic under study.
Related terms: abstract; referee.

Justification

Everyday use: to offer a good reason for a specific action or approach.
Research use: in setting out his/her research design, the researcher will use theoretical and/or empirical justifications for the proposed method, plan of work and general approach to the problem being studied.
Example: the theoretical argument for the study may be justified by reference to key texts in the literature search.
Related terms: critique; literature review; theory.

Knowledge

Everyday use: that which is known or understood.
Research use: the researcher strives to test out, modify and add to current knowledge by means of research findings.
Example: in action research, the researcher may work with a team of clinical nurses; and through a research design modify nursing interventions. If these new-style interventions are successful, their outcomes may reflect a contribution to new knowledge.
Related terms: action research; hypothesis; intervention; theory.

'Leading' question

Everyday use: leading implies taking someone in a specific direction (that is, where *you* want them to go!).

Research use: a question in an interview or questionnaire which suggests what the answer should be. 'Leading' questions introduce bias into a study. *Apparently* objective questions, such as multiple choice questions, can be 'leading' by not suggesting an appropriate or feasible alternative. The context in which a question is being asked can also influence whether or not is it is leading.

Example: 'do you believe capital punishment is an equal deterrent both to "impulse" killings and to killings occurring during carefully planned robberies?' Some respondents might not believe capital punishment has *any* deterrent effect; but their preferred response is excluded by the way in which the question is framed.

Related term: bias.

Likert scale

Everyday use: an ordinal measure of peoples' attitudes.

Research use: Likert-type scales are used to measure attitudes on an ordinal scale ranging through degrees of negative, neutral and positive responses.

Example: in an attitude scale participants were asked to respond to the statement 'Women are more sensitive to others' feelings than men' in the following categories: 'strongly agree'; 'agree'; 'undecided'; 'disagree'; 'strongly disagree'.

Related terms: attitude; measurement; scale.

Limitation

Limitation

Everyday use: a shortcoming or weakness.
Research use: a design, sampling or other problem which may limit the value of a study's findings. It is important that researchers not only identify positive outcomes; but also describe limitations that may well affect the generalising power of the study, and make suggestions for overcoming these in subsequent work.
Example: in a study of care and treatment of dangerous patients, one limitation might be that only patient samples from within assessment units were used. Acknowledgement of this limitation means that no generalisations about the findings should be made to other contexts; and it should be rectified in future studies by extending the sampling frame.
Related terms: confounding variable; generalisability; sampling frame.

Line graph

Everyday use: a method of representing numerical information graphically.
Research use: like other graphs a line graph consists of two lines at right angles to each other, known as the *axes of reference*. The horizontal line is the *x-axis* and the vertical line is the *y-axis*. Data concerning a specific variable is then plotted as a continuous line in relation to both axes. Line graphs can be used to represent several variables, though generally it is unwise to include more than six as more than this number can make the graphs hard to read and therefore lessen their impact.
Example: in discussing the Channel Four weather forecast, a presenter makes use of a line graph showing temperature changes in the last 24 hours in degrees Celsius.
Related terms: bar chart; histogram; pie chart.

Literature review

Everyday use: searching through what has been written on a particular topic.
Research use: a systematic search of published work to find out what is already known about the intended research topic. This is an early and important stage in the research process. A researcher locates papers or texts relevant to the intended study;

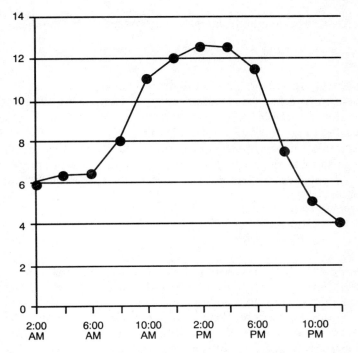

Figure 2   Line graph showing temperature changes in a
24-hour period in degrees Celsius

which may then assist in formulating the research question or
hypothesis.
Example: when studying substance abuse, relevant papers in a
library or database are collated and consulted to help determine
what is known about the subject.
Related terms: CD-ROM; database; information systems.

Literature search   *see **Literature review***

Location

Everyday use: a place or position.
Research use: in research terms location is usually referred to
in relation to the sample. It is the place where the study is being
carried out.
Example: a researcher observing the inappropriate behaviours
in an Accident and Emergency Unit identifies the Accident and
Emergency at Walsgrave Hospital. The location of the study is

therefore Accident and Emergency at Walsgrave Hospital.

Log

Everyday use: a daily record of events.
Research use: a detailed written account in which the researcher records daily events in relation to his/her study, possibly in the form of a reflective diary.
Example: in an observational study monitoring the effects of organisational change on the running of a unit or department, the researcher uses a reflective diary to describe the detailed changes he/she observes.
Related terms: data; observation.

Longitudinal study

Everyday use: monitoring a specific group through time.
Research use: a study in which data are collected about the same individuals over a long period of time. Longitudinal studies are used to measure change or continuity. They are to be contrasted with *vertical* or '*snapshot*' studies, where data are collected at a specific point and no account is taken of subsequent possible changes.
Example: an experimental team wish to record the long-term effects of a particular drug. Such a study may be ongoing in relation to possible side-effects for many years.

Mean

Everyday use: the arithmetical average of a group of scores.
Research use: used to determine the average value of a set or series of numerical data. The mean is calculated by dividing the sum of the scores by the number of individuals in the sample.
Example: in the following series of birth weights (2.9 kilos; 2.98 kilos; 3.16 kilos; 3.27 kilos; 3.3 kilos; 3.8 kilos) the mean birth weight is [2.9 + 2.98 + 3.16 + 3.27 + 3.3 + 3.8]/6 = 3.235 kilos.
Related terms: distribution; median; mode; standard deviation.

Measurement

Everyday use: describing things by attaching numbers to them.
Research use: the use of numbers to categorise or assign variables for purposes of assessment.
Example: in an observational study of administrative activities, the frequencies with which various types of paperwork occurred were recorded. These frequencies were then compared with those for other activities.
Related terms: baseline; frequency; interval scale; nominal scale; ordinal scale; range; ratio scale; scalar.

Median

Everyday use: at the middle.
Research use: a central or middle score. Used to determine the middle score, which separates the remaining scores into those

greater than, and those less than, the middle value.

Example: in the numerical series [70, 68, 66, 64, 62, 60, 58] the median score is 64, since half of the remaining scores lie above this value and half below it.

Related terms: distribution; mean; mode.

Meta-study

Everyday use: the prefix *meta-* means 'beyond'. Thus the term *meta-study* means 'beyond the (individual) study'; that is, a study involving more than one study!

Research use: a meta-study involves an analysis of several studies, all looking at various aspects of a particular problem and preferably involving different methods. The researcher examines each study in detail, looking for points of agreement or disagreement; and for the light which differing methods can shed on familiar problems. The aim is to produce a balanced conspectus and hopefully to acquire new insights from differing theoretical and practical approaches.

Example: a developmental psychologist investigating issues in language development carries out a detailed re-analysis of several classical studies on language acquisition carried out by Russian and American psychologists during the 1960s and 1970s. Looking across the studies in this way, he finds that certain issues are repeatedly cross-validated; but others; which have been broadly accepted, do not stand up to careful justification.

Related term: cross-validation.

Methodology

Everyday use: a study of methods.

Research use: methodology is not simply an account of the methods used in a particular study. It is a detailed account of the theoretical bases for such methods. A study method therefore conforms to theoretical rules, guidelines and principles outlined in the methodology.

Example: a methodological principle frequently invoked in qualitative studies is that the study does not rely on statistical data; but rather on in-depth descriptions obtained from observations and/or interviews.

Related terms: case study; experiment; interview; observation; paradigm; qualitative; survey; theory.

Methods

Everyday use: ways of doing things.
Research use: the various steps and procedures used within the research process. Strategies for gathering and analysing data usually described within the research proposal.
Example: a section of the research proposal is devoted to a description of data collection methods. Within an observational study, the researcher outlines the various techniques he/she will use to collect the observational data.
Related terms: methodology; plan of work; proposal; protocol.

Modal   *see* **Mode**

Mode

Everyday use: popular or 'fashionable'.
Research use: the modal score is the most frequently-occurring value in a set of scores.
Example: if more children at birth weighed 3.75 kilos than any other weight, then 3.75 kilos would be the modal weight for this sample.
Related terms: mean; median; standard deviation.

Model

Everyday use: a model usually refers to a small representation of something else: for example a model village; a model car; or a model railway. In the world of fashion, to 'model' an article of clothing is to show it off to best advantage.
Research use: here the term is used to indicate a ***conceptual*** representation of a theoretical proposition. Thus various aspects of larger theories may be 'modelled' in a variety of ways. Models may include (for example) practical illustrations of mathematical formulae; flow diagrams illustrating the logical implications of a theory; three-dimensional structures such as a wind-tunnel or a wave-barrier; or organic models in which the effects of agro-chemicals on soil constituents or of vulcanisation may be monitored through time.
Example: as part of a discussion on bronchial asthma, a lecturer in physiology wishes to illustrate the effects of minute changes in the diameter of a tube on the resistance it offers. He

attaches tubes of various diameters to a series of standard balloons and invites his class to try blowing them up. When they have duly noted their difficulties with the narrower tubes, he introduces the proposition that the resistance offered is inversely proportional to the square of the diameter (that is, he has 'modelled' an inverse square law of physics). His class have in fact experienced a tiny representation of the 'expulsion difficulties' encountered by asthma sufferers.

Related terms: theory; an alternative term for a model is a *paradigm*.

Modem

Everyday use: the term modem is an abbreviation for a MODulator-DEModulator device in electronics. This is a piece of hardware which allows two or more computers to communicate via the telephone network.

Research use: modems allow researchers to communicate, swap and collect information from world-wide sources, either by asking for contributions or by setting-up direct links with individuals or institutions.

Example: in developing a study on dangerous behaviours, collaborations are set up with a university in a European country. Rather than wait for long postal delays using bulky paper files, electronic versions can be transferred within minutes and responses received within a relatively short period of time. Alternatively, forums may be set up with facilities for sending and receiving immediate responses in real time.

Related terms: data; forum; hardware.

Multiple choice

Everyday use: offering a wide range of choices.

Research use: a multiple-choice test or questionnaire is a research instrument which requires the respondent to make a selection from a variety of alternative choices. Such instruments are useful in testing abilities and achievement, and also in seeking information on various attitudes or preferences within a target group.

Example: commercial vending agencies frequently use multiple-choice in requesting their potential customers to respond to some such item as the following: 'Please check the item(s) which best describe your leisure interests: 1. Gardening; 2.

Hobbies; 3. Travel; 4. Theatre; 5. Classical Music; 6. Cooking; 7. Pets; 8. Reading; 9. Outdoor; 10. New Age'.
Related terms: dichotomous response; forced-choice item.

Natural science

Everyday use: a scientific study of, or pertaining to, the natural world.
Research use: this term refers to the so-called 'basic' sciences which are concerned with describing the nature of the physical universe and of living things.
Examples: physics; chemistry; botany; zoology.
Related term: social science.

Negative skew   *see Skewness (kurtosis)*

Nominal scale

Everyday use: 'nominal' refers to naming, or attaching identifying labels to, people or things.
Research use: nominal data are data which can only be described numerically by using a nominal scale: that is, using a number to identify an individual. This is the weakest level of measurement. No arithmetical manipulations are permitted when using a nominal scale.
Example: during an observational study, patients or care staff can be identified by assigning each one a number. But it would be erroneous to try adding Patient 1 to Patient 3 and coming up with the answer Patient 4!
Related terms: interval scale; ordinal scale; ratio scale.

Non-parametric   *see Parametric*

Non-participant observation

Everyday use: the phrase implies looking without taking part.
Research use: a method of data collection in which the researchers observe the participants in their study without being themselves involved; in other words, they observe the situation 'from the outside'. This method is the opposite of *participant observation*. It may be adopted for a variety of reasons; one example being to reduce the possible risk of bias occurring as a result of participation. The researcher has a clearly-defined role which is different to that of the participants. Non-participant observers often attempt to minimise their effect on subjects by reducing their visibility.
Example: a researcher using this method to observe the dynamics of a group therapy session might choose to observe the group through a one-way mirror or remotely by video link-up.
Related terms: 'halo' effect; Hawthorn effect; participant; participant observation.

Non-responders

Everyday use: people who fail to respond.
Research use: potential subjects or informants who fail to answer or to participate in a study. The term is usually associated with questionnaire response rates. Higher levels of non-response are usually found among the elderly; rural populations; lower socio-economic groups; or 'sensitive' groups who may have been over-researched or who fear the perceived personal outcomes of the research.
Example: an acceptable response rate for questionnaires is 65 per cent or more. The remainder who do not respond are classified as non-responders.
Related term: response rate.

Norm

Everyday use: a rule or standard of social behaviour to be found within a particular population or group within a population.
Research use: in a research context the term *norm* refers to a set of scores which are characteristic of a particular, clearly defined sample. Without these scores as a reference point, it is difficult to make inferences about an individual's scores. Once a

new scale has been developed, an attempt is then made to obtain norms for it.

Example: intelligence tests all have well-developed norms, based on a mean intelligence within the general population of 100 with a standard deviation of 15.

Related terms: distribution; sample.

Normal

Everyday use: expected, usual or ordinary.

Research use: the term '*normal*' refers to a theoretical distribution of scores symmetrically around the mean; with the majority of cases (64.6 per cent) occurring within plus or minus 1 standard deviation (SD) of the mean. Many natural characteristics, such as height or weight, are distributed normally in the population.

Example: in a survey of infant health, an aim would be to achieve a representative sample by ensuring that the sample was normative – that is, not abnormally skewed in relation to weight or other important variables.

Related terms: distribution; representative; sample; skewness; standard deviation.

Normal curve   *see* **Normal distribution**

Normal distribution

Everyday use: a mathematical function (called the Gaussian distribution) which states that many variables are characteristically distributed across populations.

Research use: the **mean**, **median** and **modal** scores in a normal distribution are equal: it is therefore symmetrical. It is most commonly graphically illustrated as the bell-shaped 'normal curve'. The normal distribution can be described by its mean and its **standard deviation**. Thus some 68.26 per cent of all scores in a normal distribution will fall within one standard deviation either side of the mean. Many statistical tests are based on the assumption of normality in the distribution.

Example: national statistics are gathered to determine the normal distributions of a variety of variables such as weight and height; and health visitors assess children against these. The further away from the mean a child scores on one or other of these 'norms', the more likelihood there is of a clinical problem

occurring.
Related terms: mean; median; mode; normal; standard deviation.

Null hypothesis *see* **Hypothesis**

Objectivity

Everyday use: maintaining a balanced and unbiased approach.
Research use: the notion that research can be approached free
of subjectivity: that is, unaffected by the researcher's personal
values or feelings. Objectivity amounts to an ethical code
whereby the researcher strives to reduce the effects of bias, and
thereby to achieve a 'real' picture of the phenomena under study.
Example: in an observational study of staff activity, the
researcher attempts to record only what is happening; and to
avoid any attempts at interpretation during this phase.
Related terms: bias; ethics; reliability; subjectivity.

Observation

Everyday use: the act of watching or observing.
Research use: observation is the fundamental method in
science; and can occur at micro- or macro-levels. It can make use
of sophisticated observational aids (e.g. the microscope); or rely
on unaided visual methods. It is one of the commonest methods
of data collection. In research terms, observation refers to a
scientific approach which has a specific purpose and follows a
prescribed method.
Example: in a clinical study to determine the types of
behaviours exhibited by a particularly anxious patient, the
researcher may observe, describe and document these as they
occur. Alternatively, such behaviours may have been pre-
identified; and are then subsequently marked on a checklist as
they occur.
Related terms: questionnaire; schedule.

Observation schedule

Everyday use: a list of observations.
Research use: a research protocol which sets out in detail the procedure to be followed in collecting observational data for that particular study.
Example: in setting up a research study into parent–child interactions, the research team devise an observation schedule setting out the type and duration of observations to be made; the codes to be used; timing of breaks in observations; how to record the observations; and the duration of observational periods, together with instructions on how to use the related observation data sheet.
Related terms: data collection sheet; field notes/observations; participant observation; unstructured observation.

Open-ended

Everyday use: unrestricted; allowing a number of possible approaches.
Research use: open-ended questions are those which do not have a fixed response. When used in either questionnaire or interview designs, such questions allow participants to formulate their own answers, unrestricted by forced-choices.
Example: in a suitability study of students work placements, a typical open-ended question might read: 'How do you feel about your work placement?'
Related terms: closed question; leading question.

Ordinal scale

Everyday use: *ordinal* is an adjective derived from *order*. When we *order* something, we put it into some kind of logical arrangement (as in the phrase, 'all in order').
Research use: a scale of measurement which ranks informants according to some characteristic (e.g. height) which all possess to a greater or lesser degree (e.g. *smallest* to *largest*). The various positions on an ordinal scale are not numerically equal; and the scale is impressionistic (has impact) rather than being precise.
Example: one question appearing on a course evaluation form was the following: 'Please check the statement which you feel applies best to the course you have just undertaken: (1) It was

irrelevant to my professional needs; (2) It was only slightly relevant to my professional needs; (3) It was moderately relevant to my professional needs; (4) It was mainly relevant to my professional needs; (5) It was completely relevant to my professional needs.'

Related terms: interval scale; nominal scale; ratio scale.

p-Value

Everyday use: p (always *small* p) stands for ***probability***. Therefore it is conventional to represent the probability *under chance* of a particular occurrence by writing either p = ('probability under chance is equal to ...') or alternatively, p < ('probability under chance is less than ...'), depending on which is appropriate.

Research use: there are three conventional p-values below which an occurrence may be said to be ***statistically significant*** (that is, the probability of its occurring by chance is extremely small). These are the 5 per cent ($p < 0.05$); the 1 per cent level ($p < 0.01$); and the 0.1 per cent level ($p < 0.001$). In a research report one of these levels will be identified as the level at which the ***null hypothesis*** can be rejected. Most research in medicine follows a convention of using the 5 per cent level (that is, 1-in-20 probability of a chance occurrence).

Example: this significance level or p-value is represented as 'p < 0.05'; which in an example of this probability would mean that the null hypothesis could be rejected at the 5 per cent level of significance.

Related terms: null hypothesis; significance.

Paradigm *see **Model***

Parametric

Everyday use: conforming to certain rules or 'parameters'.

Research use: data are said to be *parametric* when they are normally distributed; selected in a genuinely random manner; when every member of the population has an equal chance of being included in the sample; and when they are measurable on an interval or ratio scale. When these conditions are met, so-called *parametric* inferential statistical tests may be used on the data; since these sophisticated tests basically assume a normal distribution. If these conditions are *not* met, then the data are said to be *non-parametric*; and distribution-free statistical tests must be used.

Example: when deciding whether or not to use a parametric test on his/her data, a researcher tests them for 'goodness of fit' to a normal distribution, possibly by inspecting a graphic layout, or by using the specific chi-squared test for this purpose.

Related terms: chi-square; distribution; 'goodness of fit'; inferential statistics; normal; population; random; sample.

Participant

Everyday use: someone who takes part.

Research use: participant is an alternative term for informants, respondents or persons taking part in a study. The term 'participant' denotes a more active role in the research process. It emphasises the relatively free nature of their collaboration with the researcher; and minimises the suggestion of control which some of the other terms carry.

Example: in an action research study, those taking part are referred to as 'participants' because of their active, formative role in the study.

Related terms: informant; respondent.

Participant observation

Everyday use: a *participant* is someone who *takes part* in an activity.

Research use: a naturalistic method of observation in which the researcher becomes a part of the naturally-occurring situation which is being studied. Everyday events are studied with the aim of understanding the participants' perspective on, and experience of, these events. The method is *participatory*, in contrast to methods or *non-participatory* observational methods. The researchers involved collect data in a more informal, unstructured and natural way. The design may be altered during the data collection phase. Thus it is considered to be a mainly qualitative method. The degree of participation can vary from full to marginal participation.

Example: in order for a researcher to find out about how a street gang operates, he lives and works with them observing their behaviours.
Related terms: ethnographic; non-participant observation.

Phenomenon

Everyday use: the word *phenomenon* is usually used to characterise a remarkable person or an event worthy of notice.
Research use: strictly speaking, a *phenomenon* can be any occurrence whatsoever. In practice, the events under study in a research programme are described as the phenomena under investigation.
Example: a researcher may set out to study the phenomena associated with an organisational change at unit level. These phenomena might include (e.g.) staff satisfaction; time available for education; amount of linguistic interaction occurring; or on-costs of change, depending on the exact focus of the study.
Related term: phenomenology.

Phenomenology

Everyday use: a study of life as it is experienced by self and others.
Research use: phenomenology is a major school of philosophy based on the view that humans are active creators of their own rules. It underpins an important branch of qualitative research, with the primary task of achieving a more essential understanding of the social and personal world.
Example: in a study of the experiences of psychiatric patients, the researcher participates as an 'in-patient' in order to try to understand the psychological effects of being 'treated' in this way.
Related terms: anthropological study; culture; existentialism; phenomenon; positivism.

Philosophy

Everyday use: the investigation of the meaning of human existence and knowledge.
Research use: relates to the study/theory of reality and the nature and meaning of existence and knowledge. Philosophy is about an individuals or societies set of beliefs which influence life

or activities. Different philosophies will determine what researchers can or cannot regard as knowledge.

Example: in justifying discussion in a research report about the behaviours of a group of people, the researcher will use existing theory which will include values and beliefs about a particular group or culture and describe the way in which knowledge was obtained (philosophy).

Related terms: culture; knowledge; phenomenology; theory.

Pie chart

Everyday use: a 'pie chart' is so called because of its obvious resemblance to an aerial view of a pie, with the various 'slices' representing differing percentages of the whole.

Research use: a pie chart is an easy and impactful way of showing the differing *proportions* or *percentages* of various characteristics represented by the data obtained in a study.

Example: in a recent survey of voting intentions in Baldersley, 40 per cent of respondents said they intended to vote Labour; 28

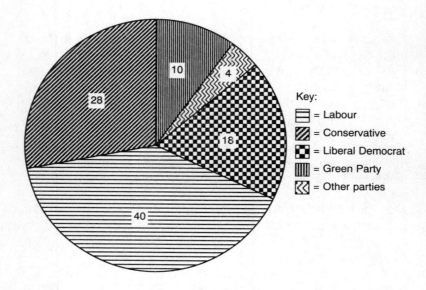

Figure 3   Voting intentions in Baldersley: pie chart to show percentage voting intentions in Baldersley at end of April 1997 (N = 1000)

per cent Conservative; 19 per cent Liberal Democrat; 10 per cent Green Party; and 4 per cent for other parties.

Related terms: bar chart; histogram; line graph; scattergram.

Placebo

Everyday use: something given instead of.

Research use: usually relates to medication or drugs whereby a substitute substance is given instead of the real medication.

Example: in an experimental design study examining the effects of a new drug one group of patients is given the real medication while the other is given a harmless lookalike substance known as the placebo.

Related terms: control group; controlled trial; experiment.

Plan of work

Everyday use: a checklist or brief written account of 'things to do'.

Research use: that part of a research proposal containing a concise statement of how the researcher proposes to carry out the study.

Example: in writing the plan of work for a research study the researcher is careful to include sections on: phases of the proposed study, their duration and what will be done during each phase; location; sampling frame; instrument(s) to be used; methods for checking reliability and validity; and practical aspects of the research.

Related term: proposal.

Population

Everyday use: normally refers to all the inhabitants of a particular country or region.

Research use: in research terms, a 'population' is the total number of individuals or things of which the research sample forms a sub-set. Thus if one were to carry out a study into attitudes of community psychiatric nurses, the *population* involved would be the total number of community psychiatric nurses currently in practice. However, since it would not be feasible to investigate the total population, a *sample* is drawn which is both representative in key features (e.g. urban/rural practice; caseload sizes) and manageable within the resources available to the study.

Related term: sample.

Positive/negative skew

Everyday use: an irregular distribution of scores within a sample and its related population.

Research use: a *positive skew* indicates that most of the extreme values are found *above* the mean (leading to an extended 'tail' of extreme values at the positive end of the distribution); and a *negative skew* means that most of the extreme values are found *below* the mean (this time the extended 'tail' is at the negative end of the distribution). This can be established by comparing the **mean** with the **median** values. For example, if the mean is greater than the median, then this suggests that over 50 per cent of the values are *below* the mean, hence giving a positive skew.

Example: in the schematic distribution shown below, the majority of scores occur leftward (*below* the mean); and there is a marked tailing-off of scores as we move rightward (*above* the mean). Hence we have a clear *positive skew*.

Related terms: mean; median; mode; normal distribution; skewness (kurtosis).

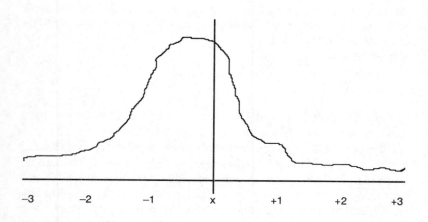

Figure 4   Schematic distribution showing positive skew

Positivism

Everyday use: 'positivist' in its extreme sense means committed to a deterministic, cause-effect view of the natural world, in which only scientific or mathematical models of reality are accepted as meaningful.

Research use: positivism is that branch of epistemology which underpins quantitative research methods. It assumes that the principles of natural science apply equally to investigative methods in the social sciences.

Example: beginning with a descriptive case study of psychiatric care at ward level, a researcher proceeds to develop the study positivistically by seeking related hypotheses and developing methods by which the data may be described quantitatively.

Related terms: descriptive research; deterministic; epistemology; hypothesis; natural science.

Practitioner research

Everyday use: implies research into a professional situation carried out by practitioners themselves.

Research use: small-scale research carried out by health practitioners within their clinical setting. This is a form of *applied research*. The aim of this form of research is to follow a research process, the outcome of which will inform practice within a specific clinical setting (that is, the setting in which the research has actually taken place). The findings of practitioner research may not be generalisable because they are specific to one setting; or because of the small scale of such projects. While such research is very unlikely to achieve the rigour of experimental research, the aim is to achieve as high a degree of rigour as is possible within the limited confines of a specific clinical setting.

Example: practitioners wishing to test out a newly created assessment instrument may wish to compare it against an existing validated instrument by testing it for *inter-rater reliability*.

Related terms: action research; applied research.

Probability

Everyday use: the likelihood that a particular event or events will occur.

Research use: the notion of probability had led to the

development of various mathematical models which are used to calculate the likelihood of different values occurring within a specified population. If a researcher knows the probability distribution of a particular variable within a population, then this allows him/her to attach a value to the test. This will act as a *parameter* (boundary) of the probability distribution (there can be more than one parameter). *Parametric* statistical tests deal with such probability distributions in situations where the data are normally distributed.

Example: if we know the mean and standard deviation for height and weight in the male population, we can calculate the probability of finding cases of obesity within that population.

Related terms: normal distribution; parametric.

Proposal

Everyday use: a suggestion or statement of intent.

Research use: the proposal or protocol is a detailed written statement describing each phase of the proposed study in terms of a recognised research process.

Example: the research proposal includes a plan of work to assist the researcher in carrying out the programme; and is usually submitted to various panels or committees for approval and funding.

Related terms: plan of work; protocol; research process.

Protocol *see* **Proposal**, for which *protocol* is an alternative term

Qualitative

Everyday use: having to do with qualities or characteristics.
Research use: qualitative research approaches belong to a family of approaches concerned with collecting in-depth data about human social contexts. They make very different assumptions about the social world than those made in quantitative research. The most striking and obvious feature is the tendency to collect data which are not numerical and hence require quite different analysis.
Example: in a qualitative study of patients' perceptions of a breast-screening programme, the focus would be to uncover the various meanings and ascriptions of the clients through a descriptive approach.
Related terms: descriptive research; ethnomethodology; phenomenology.

Qualitative analysis

Everyday use: see *qualitative method.*
Research use: analysis of qualitative data which usually takes a verbal form, having been obtained through observation or questioning techniques, or by interrogating files or archival materials. Most qualitative methods are therefore concerned with various ways of analysing *language.* They typically include *content analysis* (which involves examining the data in order to derive content categories which are valid for analysis of all the data); *critical incident analysis* (which examines the thoughts and behaviours of individuals in relation to 'key' events *see also critical analysis*); *vignette analysis* (which invokes typical professional situations as a stimulus to description); and *repertory*

grid elicitation (which asks respondents to categorise people or events according to their own individual frame of reference).

Example: a researcher wishes to find out how members of her sample categorise their workmates. She obtains a repertory of constructs from each member of the sample, based on spontaneous responses to the names of team members known to, and identified by, the respondents themselves (*repertory grid analysis*).

Related term: vignette.

Qualitative method

Everyday use: the word *qualitative* relates to qualities or characteristics which are frequently too complex to yield to simple description and require careful discussion.

Research use: the collection of such descriptive information, usually through questioning or observation. There is no single qualitative method, but rather many alternative methods. What advocates of these methods share is a rejection of simplistic empirical accounts and methods of data collection; and more importantly, of the assumptions which underlie these. Subjective data are valued; and research designs are flexible (i.e. they can develop during the process of data collection) and less formally structured than classical empirical methods. Qualitative methods and qualitative *methodology* are not identical, since the former are capable of incorporation within an overall quantitative design; while the latter implies a *study* of qualitative methods – not the methods themselves.

Example: ethnography is an example of qualitative method. While carrying out ethnographic studies of a group of people, the researcher either lives with them or spends as much time with them as possible, in an attempt to understand their values, beliefs and customs. Detailed field notes documenting these issues constitute the product of this qualitative method.

Related terms: descriptive study; ethnography; observation; questioning.

Quantitative

Everyday use: having to do with counting and numbers.

Research use: quantitative research is largely concerned with the collection of quantitative data in the form of various measures and indices; and with its description and analysis by means of statistical methods. It is basically influenced by the methods of natural science; and places great emphasis on replication and verifiability.

Example: in a study classifying therapeutic interventions occurring with a large sample of patients, a researcher uses a twenty-item checklist. He/she then rates the characteristics of each interaction numerically on an ordinal scale within each classifying item. At this stage, the researcher may be less interested in the qualitative aspects of individual interactions than in their numerical frequencies and defined values.

Related terms: frequency; inferential statistics; natural science; ordinal.

Quantitative analysis

Everyday use: a method of investigation or assessment involving the use of numbers.

Research use: quantitative analysis involves use of one or more of a variety of techniques available for the statistical analysis of data. These can range from basic *descriptive statistics* involving frequencies, range, mean or modal scores, variance or standard deviation, through to sophisticated methods using *inferential statistics* to assess the probability under chance of a specific result being obtained.

Example: a researcher wishing to offer a simple description of factual data obtained during a survey of wheelchair users may use such descriptive indices as the total frequency of users; their distribution by region in the UK; the range of wheelchairs in use; and the frequency of wheelchairs on loan from public and voluntary sources.

Related term: qualitative analysis.

Quasi-experimental

Everyday use: emulating – but not exactly like – an experiment.

Research use: quasi-experimental studies are those which attempt to adopt the methods of a truly experimental study in a real setting, such as an everyday clinical or treatment context. Typically they experience difficulties of control and selectivity, which the researchers seek to minimise. Quasi-experimental studies are examples of quantitative research. For a variety of reasons – theoretical, methodological, ethical and because of the sheer complexity of social life, social researchers cannot often apply true experimental conditions within their studies.

Example: in studying the effects of a specific therapy, the researcher seeks to match or balance the groups studied, and to obtain a control group, without frankly interfering in the daily therapeutic process.

Related terms: control group; experiment.

Questionnaire

Everyday use: a list of questions on a specific topic.

Research use: an instrument designed to deliver a series of well-formulated written questions, distributed either in person or by mail. Typically used to gather large amounts of data in extensive samples whose members are relatively inaccessible or expensive to reach for purposes of interview.

Example: a health researcher uses a questionnaire to carry out a large-scale survey of wheelchair users to determine whether they are satisfied with their current wheelchairs; and if not, what modifications they would find useful.

Related terms: instrument; interview; response rate; sample; survey.

Random

Everyday use: haphazard − something that occurs unpredictably without any prearranged order.
Research use: in large-scale studies, random selection of informants from a suitable sampling frame increases the likelihood of obtaining valid results.
Example: a researcher involved in health promotion selects his/her sample for a health education intervention by consulting a random-number table in a book of statistical tables.
Related term: sample.

Random error

Everyday use: a haphazard mistake.
Research use: a mistake made in, or during, data collection; an error in measurement. It is assumed that error *always* occurs when some form of measurement takes place in research. However, because of the random nature of this type of error, there is a tendency for it to be self-correcting; and bias is unlikely to occur in any particular direction.
Example: if errors are made in recording speeds at which some subjects complete a task, then there is an equal likelihood that errors will *overestimate* and *underestimate* the actual speed. Any average is therefore likely to be accurate.
Related terms: random; randomisation.

Randomisation

Everyday use: the random assignment of subjects to particular groups in a study.

Random number

Research use: randomisation is a powerful means of controlling for both recognised and unrecognised factors which might affect or confound results. Randomisation can also occur within a study, for example by randomly assigning the order in which subjects receive different treatments or conditions.

Example: a randomised control trial will randomly assign subjects to different conditions, one being a ***control group*** in which no intervention occurs. Changes in experimental group subjects are compared with those occurring in the control.

Related terms: control group; experimental group; random sampling; sample; stratified.

Random number

Everyday use: one of a series of numbers having no detectable pattern.

Research use: random numbers, or rather tables of random numbers, are used to create simple random samples. Such tables are often found as an appendix in research or statistical textbooks.

Example: in a study observing nurse and patient interactions, there are a total of six nurses being observed. Each nurse is assigned one of these numbers as his/her code. Random-number sequences for observation may be generated by a computer or (more informally) picked out of a hat. Numbers of randomised observation sequences for three sets of observations may be, for example, 5–3–6–1–2–4: 1–3–2–5–4–6: and 4–6–1–5–3–2.

Related terms: random; random sampling.

Random sampling

Everyday use: the process of selecting a sample for a study which will be representative of the population in question.

Research use: random sampling means that any member of the population in question has an equal chance of being chosen for the study. There are three commonly used methods of selecting a random sample: systematic selection; selection by lottery; and selection by random numbers.

Example: clinical drug trials (experimental) most commonly use this design.

Related terms: random; randomisation; random number.

Range

Everyday use: the total span of anything.
Research use: this statistic identifies the dispersion of values or scores in a series of values, from lowest to highest.
Example: in a series of values with a highest score of 92 and a lowest score of 42, the range is given by [92 – 42] = 50.
Related term: dispersion.

Ranked

Everyday use: arranged in an hierarchal order.
Research use: for descriptive purposes, scores are sometimes 'ranked' in order of ascending value to facilitate the use of non-parametric statistical tests.
Example: in the numerical series [3, 5, 7, 9, 11] the numbers would be allocated ranks 1 to 5 respectively. In the case of tied scores, each score is allocated an appropriate fractional rank. Thus, if the series were [3, 5, 5, 7, 9, 11], the ranks allocated would be [1, 2.5, 2.5, 3, 4, 5].
Related terms: non-parametric; ordinal.

Ranking

Everyday use: the arranging of items in order.
Research use: ranking scales are commonly used in research by social scientists where subjects will be asked to arrange items in a rank order, perhaps arranging in order or preference, rather than selecting a particular item.
Example: the ranking by individuals of the fastest modes of transport to determine the trends in which people perceive are the fastest. This may be done using a scale of 1 (slow) to 5 (fast) and the following modes would be placed in order. Car, Bus, Cycle, Horse, Air Balloon.
Related terms: nominal scale; ordinal scale.

Rating

Everyday use: the assignment of a numerical value to an observation, judgement or assessment.
Research use: rating in social science research commonly takes the form of use of rating scales, in which respondents are asked to rate items which tell the researcher something

concerning that individual's perceptions of a particular issue. *Self-rating* instruments allow the respondent to rate him/herself on (for example) a quality, attitude or personality trait.

Example: the following is an item drawn from a simple forced-choice perceptual rating scale: 'Which of the following professionals do you consider to be the most caring? Nurse; Policeman; Traffic Warden; Solicitor.'

Related term: ranking.

Ratio scale

Everyday use: the relationship between two or more values.

Research use: a descriptive statistic frequently very useful in illustrative comparisons of numerical data. The ratio of one number to another is given by dividing one number by the other.

Example: in a study it was found that patients categorised as 'psychologically disordered', when compared to those categorised as 'mentally ill', used the hospital facilities to a significantly greater extent (i.e. in a ratio of 2:1).

Related term: descriptive statistic.

Raw score

Everyday use: naturally occurring or 'untreated'.

Research use: scores or other data which have been collected, but not as yet coded, sorted or statistically treated in any way. Such 'raw' data are subsequently analysed either statistically or by various qualitative methods such as discourse or content analysis.

Example: returned questionnaires, with their untreated responses, would constitute raw data. Similarly, verbatim transcripts of audiotaped interviews are the raw data from which subsequent interpretations will be made.

Related terms: content analysis; discourse analysis; qualitative; statistical analysis.

Reductionism

Everyday use: 'the whole is simply the sum of its parts.'

Research use: an attempt to understand complex phenomena by studying the constituent parts of which they consist.

Example: studying organisms by analysing their chemical structures, behaviours or physiological responses. Studying

groups by analysing the behaviour of individuals.
Related terms: behaviour; positivism.

Referee

Everyday use: an official who is there to see 'fair play'. An official whose opinion is requested in the event of a dispute.
Research use: an experienced researcher to whom research proposals, funding requests, progress reports and academic papers are referred for peer review.
Example: when any research proposal is submitted to a public or voluntary authority with a request for funding, the organisation will refer the proposal to a referee of its choice for his/her opinion on the potential value of the work and the appropriateness of the method(s) selected.

Reflective technique

Everyday use: when we 'reflect' we mull over our past experiences.
Research use: reflective techniques are used to encourage respondents to remember past events and experiences which may be important sources of data for the study concerned; and/or to validate data previously obtained from respondents. Techniques include asking people to recall *specific incidents*; use of **vignettes** to stimulate professional interest; use of *photographs* or other pictorial materials; and inviting respondents to keep a *reflective diary*.
Example: in the early stages of a study on stress, a researcher carries out videotaped interviews with members of his sample. Later, the videotapes are played back to respondents so that they may verify the content after a period of reflection.
Related term: vignette.

Regression

Everyday use: a tendency to move towards the 'average'.
Research use: this is based on the tendency for scores to *regress* towards the arithmetic mean. Knowing how much regression towards the mean occurs for a specific pair of variables enables one to predict reasonably accurately, especially when the regression is minimal.
Example: very tall people tend to have children somewhat

taller (closer to the mean); and very short people tend to have children somewhat shorter (closer to the mean). The extent of this regression offers a likely prediction of future heights in the family.

Related terms: correlation; regression analysis.

Regression analysis

Everyday use: finding out how pronounced is the tendency to move towards 'the average' in a given group of scores.

Research use: based on statistical techniques for explaining or predicting the *spread* or ***dispersion*** of a dependent variable. Used to establish a mathematical equation to indicate the relationship between variables. The number in the regression equation that indicates the values of an independent variable is known as the *regression coefficient*.

Example: if we found that, for every year spent in a psychiatric hospital, patient assaults increased by five, then the regression coefficient would be five.

Related terms: correlation; dispersion; regression.

Related groups

Everyday use: groups of subjects that share similar characteristics.

Research use: used to study a variable that is not attributable to differences between groups.

Example: studying reading ability in a pre-/post-test design, when one group have received instruction and the other have not, would require that both groups were similar in all other characteristics.

Related terms: correlation; relationship.

Relationship

Everyday use: the way in which one phenomenon is related to another.

Research use: used to establish the way in which one variable corresponds or contrasts with another.

Example: in the study of cardiovascular disease, *high cholesterol* and *coronary atheroma* have been demonstrated to be *related* variables.

Related term: correlation.

Relationship frequency distribution

Everyday use: a percentage proportion.
Research use: used to show the average in relation to the overall construct.
Example: if sickness at work was on average fifty-four days of the year, their *relative frequency* would be given by the formula **0.15 x (54/365)**: that is, the percentage of days on which sickness occurred would be 15 per cent.
Related terms: relationship; relative frequency.

Relative frequency

Everyday use: a number of things seen in relation to the total number.
Research use: a descriptive statistic derived by dividing the frequency displaying a particular characteristic by the total frequency.
Example: if it rained on 36 days each year, the relative frequency with which rain occurred would be [36/365] = 1.01.
Related term: frequency.

Reliability

Everyday use: the extent to which something can be relied upon to do its job properly.
Research use: the extent to which repeated measures using the same instrument will give similar results (*test–retest reliability*). Any data collection instrument (e.g. interview schedule; questionnaire; scale) should display reasonable reliability in this respect; otherwise some re-design may be necessary. A high positive correlation with subsequent scores indicates a high level of test–retest reliability.
Example: if you were going to weigh a number of people, you would be wise to check the reliability of the scales by standing on them yourself a number of times. If the scales give a similar reading each time, they may be regarded as reliable (though they may not be accurate!). In research terms, administering a questionnaire to the same individuals following a suitable interval will provide a useful measure of its reliability.
Related term: validity.

Reliability coefficient

Everyday use: a measure of the extent to which results obtained can be relied upon.

Research use: a mathematical test of the consistency of a research instrument. The reliability coefficient is a correlational statistic which indicates how reliable an instrument is. The coefficient can range through negative numbers (indicating an inverse relationship) through zero (no reliability) to unity (complete reliability).

Example: questions on a survey instrument are evaluated by two independent raters and their level of agreement can be measured by calculation of a reliability coefficient.

Related terms: correlation; reliability.

Re-measure

Everyday use: the same group of informants are given the same test on two or more occasions.

Research use: a research method which measures the same group on a number of occasions to assess change or differences over time. The informants are, in effect, their own control group.

Example: a group of informants are tested for reading ability and then undertake a course of reading practice, following which they are tested again.

Related terms: control; test–retest.

Repertory grid

Everyday use: the word *repertory* is derived from *repertoire*: both words meaning a range of activities or ideas.

Research use: repertory grid is a technique devised by the American psychologist, G.A. Kelly. It relates to his theory of *personal constructs* which regards human beings as essentially problem solvers, who categorise or construct their reality on the basis of significant past events. These constructs are elicited by inviting an individual to categorise significant persons, events or situations in his/her life along self-generated continua.

Example: a researcher is interested in lecturers' perceptions regarding the characteristics of good teachers. He/she invites each respondent to think about the members of his/her teaching team and to think of ways in which its various members are similar to, and different from, each other. In this way a series of evaluative

continua based on critical personal criteria are devised.
Related term: qualitative method.

Replication study

Everyday use: the act of repeating something.
Research use: the process of replicating (or attempting to re-run) a completed study, either to increase confidence in its findings, or to develop or refute them. Repeating a study with different informants is one method of improving the external validity of a study by 'pooling' resultant data.
Example: research findings that a specific drug relieved pain would be more readily accepted if it could be shown to relieve pain in a number of different settings and on a number of different occasions.
Related terms: external validity; generalisability.

Representative

Everyday use: similar to the whole.
Research use: the generalisability of a study's findings to other groups or situations. Representativeness is an important goal of sampling technique. A genuinely representative sample can be used to draw inferences about the total population from which it is drawn.
Example: a sufficiently large, random stratified sample drawn from all the forensic nurses working in special hospitals and Regional Secure Units may reasonably be regarded as *representative* of the total population of employed forensic nurses. By contrast, partial samples, taken from one or two such locations only, would not be a genuinely representative sample of all employed forensic nurses.
Related terms: population; sample.

Research

Everyday use: a process of study and/or investigation.
Research use: the systematic investigation of a subject aimed at uncovering new information. Research can be undertaken in many different ways and at either theoretical or empirical level.
Examples: these can include research in the natural and social sciences; descriptive research into various belief systems (epistemic, ethical) and researches into language, music and the

fine arts.
Related terms: design; hypothesis; method.

Research design

Everyday use: the method of planning research to gather the most appropriate information, in the correct way, and to analyse the results effectively.
Research use: a series of stages used in the research process to enable the researcher to build up a precise and systematic plan or blueprint of work to be done.
Example: during Phase 1 in the design of an action research programme the researcher may develop research instruments and carry out pilot work. Phase 2 may involve determining the location and sample; carrying out main data collection; interpretation of the findings; and development of a planned programme of change. Phase 3 may involve carrying out the change programme; re-measuring the relevant variables; and carrying out the final analysis. Finally, Phase 4 may include writing the final report and appropriate dissemination of the work.
Related terms: plan of work; proposal.

Research process

Everyday use: the method or stages in carrying out research.
Research use: used to apply scientific rigour to the understanding of a problem.
Example: the accepted way of conducting scientific research, by the process of theoretical argument; data collection; analysis of results; and interpretation of findings.
Related terms: methods; research design.

Respondent

Everyday use: somebody who 'responds'.

Retrospective data

Everyday use: retrospective means 'looking backwards' (that is, into the past).
Research use: data obtained during research carried out on events that have already occurred. Usually used where there are records or documentary evidence from which variables or themes

can be extracted.

Example: in a study examining the components of company records, a documentary analysis is carried out examining each discrete component within them.

Related term: historical research.

Right of refusal

Everyday use: the right of individuals to say no.

Research use: specifically, the right of individuals to refuse when asked if they wish to participate in research. An ethical principle in research which establishes the participation in a study as *voluntary*.

Example: in a study which asks patients about their care and treatment, some patients may feel that they do not wish to take part either because they simply do not want to; or because they may feel threatened or anxious that if they speak out it may affect their treatment. Right of refusal can be invoked at any time during the study by the informant terminating the interview.

Related terms: ethics; informed consent.

Rigour

Everyday use: in-depth examination.

Research use: research is carried out with rigour to ensure that it is exact and precise. Such rigour therefore tries to eliminate any bias or misinterpretation striving towards critical analysis.

Example: in a study examining washing powder preference, there may be a number of reasons why brand X or Y is preferred. For example, price or availability may be factors that influence choice as well as the quality of the wash. The research will be more rigorous if the researcher includes these factors in his study.

Related terms: critical analysis; systematic.

Sample

Everyday use: a part used for purposes of testing the whole.
Research use: a group of informants selected from a larger group in the hope that they are representative of the larger group in the variable(s) under study. If this is the case, then studying the sample can reveal potentially important information about the population from which it is drawn.
Example: studying a sample of midwives should produce generalisable data concerning their attitudes and approaches which are in some ways true of all midwives.
Related terms: generalisability; population; representative; sampling frame.

Sampling

Everyday use: taking a proportion of subjects from a larger population.
Research use: used to reflect the generalisability of effects observed in the chosen group to the larger population.
Example: in a marketing survey (examining views of a shop product), choosing a *systematic sample* (e.g. every fifth person walking into a shop) and asking him/her to be an informant would ensure that people are represented from different backgrounds, cultures and age groups.
Related terms: random sample; sample.

Sampling bias

Everyday use: an error which means that the sample does not reflect the larger population from which it was chosen.

Sampling distribution

Research use: used to express the extent to which the findings are not generalisable.
Example: asking a sample of passers-by in a staunch Conservative area about their political loyalties and voting intentions prior to a General Election is unlikely accurately to reflect the views of the total British electorate.
Related term: sampling error.

Sampling distribution

Everyday use: the way the scores fall in any set of results.
Research use: how the scores from a specific sample are ordered. It is used to arrange the data to facilitate analysis.
Example: measuring the blood pressure of all men aged between 35 and 50 years working in a specific company could materially help to establish national norms. The data could be arranged from highest to lowest in systolic and diastolic phases. This ordering could then be 'pooled' with similar data to help establish population norms.
Related terms: frequency; norm; sample.

Sampling error

Everyday use: the extent of error in sampling.
Research use: a statistical measure to represent the amount of error in a research sample.
Example: if one were to ask 100 factory staff if they had ever misused equipment, and 30 per cent said they had, this may be a close enough sample of the entire population of factory staff. However, suppose the figure was 'out' by 5 per cent, the true figure could vary between 25 and 35 per cent. The sampling error here would therefore be plus or minus 5 per cent.
Related term: sampling bias.

Sampling frame

Everyday use: the group from which your sample will be chosen.
Research use: a carefully defined description of the 'eligible group' from which the study sample will be selected.
Example: if, in surveying staff morale, you decided to question every fifth driver parking his/her car in the car park, the total number of cars parked there on a defined occasion would

constitute the sampling frame. Note that this sampling frame does *not* include the total number of *staff*, since some may not have cars.

Related terms: population; sample.

Scale/scalar

Everyday use: an instrument used to weigh or measure a quality or attribute (e.g. weight, height, density). The term *scalar* is an adjective meaning *having the properties of, or related to, a scale*. Scalar data are data which can be arranged in a logical order or sequence.

Research use: scales can vary between the finely calibrated, highly accurate instruments used in the natural sciences and the more global, verbal instruments typically used in the social sciences.

Examples: physical scales (e.g. manometer; micrometer screwgauge; haemocytometer; sphygmomanometer): psychological scales (e.g. Wechsler Intelligence Scale for Children (WISC); Wechsler Adult Intelligence Scale (WAIS); Minnesota Multiphasic Personality Inventory (MMPI); Eysenck Personality Inventory (EPI); General Health Questionnaire (GHQ)).

Related terms: calibration; interval scale; nominal scale; ordinal scale; ratio scale.

Scatter/scattergram

Everyday use: the pattern produced by plotting two or more variables on a graph.

Research use: the pattern produced by the graph indicates the strength and direction of any relationship(s) between the variables.

Example: height and weight are two closely correlated variables which might be plotted in this way to produce a scattergram within which any anomalies would be readily detectable.

Related terms: correlation; variable.

Schedule

Everyday use: a schedule is some form of orderly list.

Research use: typically a list setting out the order and format of questions to be asked during a research interview. Alternatively

Science

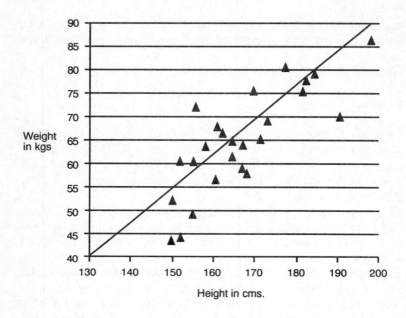

Figure 5   Scattergram showing positive correlational
pattern of height and weight (N = 25)

it may be a checklist of research activities to be completed during
a typical data collection session.
Example: an interview schedule may be very detailed or only
indicate broad areas for questions. Specific questions in a survey of
staff morale might include: 'What do you feel is the main cause of
low staff morale?' or 'What helps to promote high staff morale?'
Related term: interview.

Science

Everyday use: (1) the process of gaining knowledge by
systematic study; (2) a body of accumulated expert knowledge.
Research use: investigation of the natural and social world by
empirical methods, with observation and questioning as its two
fundamental methods. Natural sciences study the properties of the
natural world (e.g. physics; chemistry; biology). Social sciences
focus on the study of human culture and interaction (e.g.
anthropology; sociology; psychology).

Example: in a behavioural study, the contingencies surrounding a particular maladaptive behaviour are observed to determine which environmental factors are reinforcing the behaviour.
Related terms: descriptive; empirical; hypothesis; theory.

Scientific

Everyday use: of, or pertaining to, the pursuit of science. A person who carries out scientific research within a specific scientific discipline is known as a *scientist*.
Research use: adjective related to 'science', indicating systematic study and the precise, logical, sequenced stages by which a scientific investigation is carried out. Systematic and rigorous steps to ensure that research is credible and worthwhile.
Example: typical scientific research involves testing hypotheses by the collection, analysis and interpretation of research data.
Related term: science.

Score

Everyday use: to keep a record.
Research use: in order to keep a record of something the researcher marks a record or makes a note of something that happens. This may be a tally (making a mark every time something happens). Adding these together creates a score.
Example: during data collection a researcher uses a Likert type scale to record what people think about a food product. Using a 5 point Likert type scale liking the product would be a score of 1 through to not liking it which would be a score of 5. Adding these scores up would indicate, for example, the higher the score, the less people would like the product.
Related terms: frequency; questionnaire.

Secondary data

Everyday use: 'second-hand' data; not original.
Research use: data obtained in studies previously completed by self or others, which are now used to inform a further empirical investigation, or as a subject of further critical study.
Example: in carrying out a critical study of the work of Sigmund Freud, the researcher would use both primary data

obtained from the writings of Freud himself; and secondary data obtained from previous critical writings about Freud carried out by others.

Related terms: critical analysis; direct (primary) data.

Secondary source

Everyday use: 'secondary sources' are information sources where other people's work, ideas or activities are described by someone else.

Research use: someone else describing or analysing data which have previously been collected, analysed and described by others. This process is known as *secondary analysis*. Secondary sources are extensively employed during literature surveys and validation studies (validity).

Example: a nurse researcher preparing to carry out a study on systematic approaches to care writes an extensive literature survey describing previous work in the field.

Related term: direct (primary) data.

Selective sample

Everyday use: being 'selective' implies the wish to be careful about which individuals or things are included.

Research use: a selective sample is one which is non-random: that is, its members have been selected because of their special suitability to yield the type(s) of data required by the study.

Example: if a researcher is conducting a survey of public satisfaction with day care facilities, then he/she would be well advised to draw a *selective sample* of individuals who have actually used such services, or who have experience of them in some other capacity. Though otherwise members of the general public, such selected individuals will be especially appropriate informants because of that special experience.

Related term: sample.

Self-report techniques

Everyday use: self-report implies telling someone about oneself.

Research use: used to provide information regarding an informant's view of him/herself. Research methods that involve the informants completing questionnaires about themselves and their perceptions, feelings or opinions.

Example: in a study of hostility, a series of statements that require true or false answers are completed by self report: for example, 'Do you get upset easily?'
Related terms: dichotomous response; questionnaire; response rate.

Semi-structured interview

Everyday use: an interview in which the questions asked are broad and allow for a degree of flexibility.
Research use: used to explore issues which are complex and generally do not lend themselves to 'cut-and-dried' answers. The researcher is free to prompt the subject with additional information or probe questions.
Example: in a study examining workers' perceptions of health and safety at work the researcher may ask: 'Could you tell me about the introduction you had to health and safety?' Spontaneous probes or prompts may include (for example): 'Who introduced it?'; 'Did you get enough support when it was introduced?'; 'What were you first impressions of it?'
Related terms: interview; interview schedule.

Set theory

Everyday use: a set is a series of events, objects or numbers which are distinguishable in some way from others (i.e. they form a 'set').
Research use: set theory is a branch of mathematical logic which deals with the characteristics of, and relations between, sets.
Example: if you collect data on all murders (defined as the intentional illegal killing of persons, as contrasted with all other causes of death), then the murdered group would constitute a set.
Related terms: data; theory.

Significance/significant

Everyday use: meaningfulness or importance.
Research use: normally refers to statistical significance. This occurs when the probability of a given numerical difference or relationship occurring by chance alone is equal to, or less than, 0.05 ($p < 0.05$). The statistical significance of results increases as their probability decreases. The conventional cut-offs are:

significant (p < 0.05); very significant (p < 0.01); highly significant (p < 0.001 or less). (NB: Numerical results can be statistically significant, yet have no practical significance. The latter depends very much on their meaningfulness – or lack of it – in relation to the issue being studied.)

Example: in an observational study, the frequencies of specific behaviours are recorded and a statistical test (chi-squared) applied to assess whether the frequencies with which certain behaviours occur differ significantly from other behavioural frequencies.

Related terms: chi-square; frequency; probability.

Skewness (kurtosis)

Everyday use: to be 'skewed' is to be deformed or pushed out of shape.

Research use: refers to a distribution whose shape differs from the normal bell-shaped curve (normal distribution), because the scores are 'bunched' together either above or below the mean, producing a degree of shift in the resultant curve. When plotted on a graph, the scores produce a non-symmetrical curve.

Example: a battery of intelligence tests is given to a group of ten-year-olds of high ability. Because many of the children are above-average ability, the resultant curve is positively skewed (i.e. results cluster well above mean values).

Related terms: cluster analysis; distribution.

Social science

Everyday use: a scientific study of social phenomena; science applied to the solution of social problems.

Research use: a term applied to any of the sciences dealing with social phenomena: for example, psychology; sociology; political science; economics. Each social science has its own well-developed code of research design and analysis. The social sciences deal characteristically (though not exclusively) with observational and questioning data, often collected by means of interviews and/or questionnaires. Unlike the natural sciences, the data of the social sciences tends to be 'soft', or qualitative, in nature.

Example: terms such as psychology and sociology are all-embracing; and each social science includes numerous sub-sets. For example, psychology may itself be sub-divided into (*inter alia*) philosophical psychology; historical psychology;

developmental psychology; clinical psychology; physiological psychology; cognitive psychology; forensic psychology and social psychology.
Related term: natural science.

Sociogram

Everyday use: a symbolic diagram related to a social group.
Research use: a graphic representation of relations among individuals. It displays their relationships and interactions constructed on the basis of an appropriate sociometric measure (sociometry).
Example: answers to the question, 'Who would you most like to work with?' for six people could be represented by drawing linking lines between letters or numbers symbolising the six people concerned.
Related term: sociometry.

Sociometry

Everyday use: the word implies 'measurement of social behaviour'.
Research use: research methods which facilitate investigation of peoples' preferred patterns of social interaction with others. The results of such a study may be presented in the form of a *sociogram* (that is, a flowchart showing the preferred interaction patterns in graphic form).
Example: as part of a team-building exercise, a unit manager carries out a study to determine the preferred working partnerships currently existing among his staff.

'Soft' data

Everyday use: colloquially used, 'soft' means, comfortable, easier to handle, more user-friendly. It also carries the somewhat disparaging nuance of 'lacking in rigour'.
Research use: data obtained by using qualitative research methods that tend not to use numbers. Used predominantly to refer to qualitative research data.
Example: research into nurses' perceptions of nursing interventions may ask a series of questions relating to the type and nature of interactions with patients. This would generate

qualitative-descriptive details which would be regarded as soft data.

Related terms: descriptive research; qualitative.

Software

Everyday use: programs that run on a computer.
Research use: computer packages which assist in managing data.
Example: databases may be used to input data which can be utilised to store and analyse data extremely efficiently. Other examples of software are: statistical packages; graphics packages; and word-processing programs.
Related term: hardware.

Spearman correlation test

Everyday use: 'correlation' generally implies looking for some form of relationship between two or more sets of figures.
Research use: an inferential statistical test used to examine relationships between two or more sets of non-parametric data.
Example: researchers studying nurse–patient relationships and shared activities find similar results within several wards. Use of the Spearman test would assist in determining the statistical relationship in between the various sets of scores.
Related terms: correlation; non-parametric; significance.

Spreadsheet

Everyday use: computer software which produces a matrix for managing numbers.
Research use: numerical data collected during a research program may be entered directly into a spreadsheet, where a whole range of quantitative techniques may be applied to it with rapidity and ease.
Example: members of a research team investigating 'hyperactive' behaviour in children using psychometric sub-scales with repeated measures are able to 'pool' large amounts of data by entering the scores serially into a customised spreadsheet. By this means, scores are available for instant analysis at any stage of the study.

Standard deviation

Everyday use: the average difference from the mean shown by a group of scores.

Research use: a statistic which shows the amount of dispersion occurring in a group of scores. It is given by taking the square root of the variance; or may be obtained directly by using the following equation:

$$SD = \sum[x{-}M]^2 / [N{-}1]$$

where $\sum$ tells us to sum all the individual $[x{-}M]^2$s in the sample; x represents an individual score; M is the sample mean; and N is the sample size.

Example: the standard deviation is closely related to the variance. Thus if we consider two groups of scores, one having a variance of 60 and the second a variance of only 20, the standard deviation will be greater in the first group.

Related terms: dispersion; statistics; variance.

Standard score *see Z-score*

Statistical analysis *see Quantitative analysis*

Statistically significant *see Significance*

Statistics

Everyday use: numerical summaries of data of various kinds.

Research use: (1) a numerical index describing a collective characteristic of a set of data (e.g. mean, median, mode, standard deviation); the study of such characteristics is known as descriptive statistics; (2) a branch of mathematics discussing probability and employing inferential tests to assess numerical relationships and probabilities affecting data (inferential statistics).

Example: data measurable on interval or ratio scales may be described in terms of 'standard' statistical characteristics (mean, median, mode, range and so on). Similarly, various inferential tests (e.g. chi-squared) may be applied to data which are partitioned in various ways.

Related terms: chi-square; interval scale; mean; median; mode; probability; ratio scale; standard deviation.

Stratification

Everyday use: organised in layers or strata.
Research use: social stratification (i.e. the structure of social groups or classes in a society) is frequently used in sampling theory to produce a so-called *stratified sample*, which seeks to reflect the proportions of various social groups present in the population as a whole.
Example: in a study of relative affluence, a stratified random sample based on occupational status might be used.
Related terms: population; random; sample.

Stratified non-random sample

Everyday use: implies a sample which is selected rather than random, but with some attempt to represent sub-groups.
Research use: a quota of subjects chosen from a sub-group or sub-groups for convenience, when larger numbers are not available for random selection.
Example: in the study described above, a researcher may be limited to quotas drawn from a limited number of settings in the local health authority. Therefore his/her nursing sub-groups, though stratified, would be non-random in nature.
Related terms: sampling; sampling bias; sampling frame; stratified random sample.

Stratified random sample

Everyday use: a sample of people or things randomly chosen from a sub-group of a total population.
Research use: used to ensure a representative sample.
Example: the total research population might be all nurses practising in a given health authority; and the sub-group might be all nursing auxiliaries, enrolled nurses, or registered nurses so practising.
Related terms: sample; stratified non-random sample.

Structured interview

Everyday use: an interview with a definite shape and structure.
Research use: a formal research interview which follows a set pattern of questions, and offers a fixed set of response options.

It is akin to the questionnaire; but is conducted 'face-to-face'. Because the responses of interviewees are constrained by the structure of the instrument, data are more objective and more easily tabulated and analysed.

Example: such an approach might be employed to measure satisfaction with services for a given population. Questions could focus on a range of identified areas (for example food; staff attitudes; range of activities); with responses limited to YES or NO. With an interview done in this way, the researcher is able to explain and clarify any difficulties, and overcome the problem of non-response with relative ease.

Related terms: questionnaire; schedule; unstructured interview.

Subject

Everyday use: the person or issue being studied.
Research use: an individual being studied as a source of data. The 'individual' can be a person, but may also be a cell, a gas molecule, a city, a mode of transport, or any other stipulated datum.
Example: someone or something so studied.
Related terms: data; informant; respondent.

Subjective/subjectivity

Everyday use: personal; to do with the individual.
Research use: relates to the (often unconscious and unintended) intrusion of personal ideas, values and emotions into the research process. In a positive sense, subjectivity may help researchers gain access to the personal meanings which individuals use to construct their reality. More negatively, subjectivity may result in the introduction of personal bias on the part of the researcher.
Example: if a researcher wishes to explore a sensitive issue such as discrimination in the Health Service, subjective impressions gained from respondents become a valuable source of data. However, the analysis and interpretation of such data pose methodological problems if the scientific requirement of objectivity is to be upheld.
Related term: objectivity.

Summated scale

Everyday use: anything 'summated' has been added up – therefore this refers to the sum total of all the scores.
Research use: refers to the total scores where individual items on a rating scale have been assigned a value. Scaling techniques are commonly used in the measurement of attitudes.
Example: a researcher may wish to measure the attitudes of care staff toward the mentally ill. Respondents would be asked to indicate their level of agreement with a series of positive and negative statements about the mentally ill, on an ordinal scale ranging, for example, from *strongly agree* to *strongly disagree*. Each item will be assigned a value (score), the total of which provides a summated rating.
Related terms: Likert scale; ordinal scale.

Survey

Everyday use: an extensive review.
Research use: usually a large-scale research design in which a sample of informants is drawn from a given population. The survey is used to draw inferences concerning the population. Surveys are typically non-interventive and do not conform to experimental design.
Example: the British Decennial Census (occurring every ten years).
Related terms: design; inference; intervention; population; sample.

Systematic

Everyday use: a step by step approach.
Research use: a regular plan of work that has a multi-stage approach. The research process is systematic because of its logical steps, e.g. literature review, methods and design, piloting, data collection, analysis and report writing.
Example: in a review of the literature for a research programme the researcher systematically reviews the subject under study. This will involve searching databases for text relating to the project, reviewing their appropriateness, critiquing the methods used and examining their findings.
Related terms: research process; scientific.

Systematic error

Everyday use: an error which is likely to be regularly repeated because its cause is 'built into' the situation.

Research use: these are errors which can occur for a variety of reasons, or even due to an accumulation of reasons. Such causes may include (for example) interviewer effects; interviewer bias; or faults in instruments used for measuring. Because these errors are likely to occur in one particular direction and are hard to detect, they are likely to influence outcome and are a threat to validity.

Example: a researcher interviewing informants might introduce systematic errors by giving additional prompts (not contained in the interview schedule) to certain individuals – for example, those whom the researcher considers to be less able to give appropriate answers.

~ T ~

Target group

Everyday use: people or situations forming a focus or 'target'.
Research uses: (1) the population about which it is hoped to make inferences following the study: (2) colleagues or fellow-workers having an interest in this particular field of study, and to whom written papers and/or reports will be directed.
Example: in a study of failure to take up maternal health care opportunities, the target groups will be (1) the mothers falling into the non-takeup category; (2) the GPs, nurses and other health care workers involved in this area of work.
Related terms: inference; population.

Test–retest reliability   *see* **Reliability**

Theme

Everyday use: may be *either* an interpretation that emerges from a data set; *or* a set of theoretical propositions which guide the construction of a research project.
Research use: used as a framework for collecting and interpreting data.
Example: there has been a thematic shift in recent research on sexual abuse and violence from a **reductionist** approach towards a broader *sociological* approach.
Related term: analysis.

Theory

Everyday use: a general statement about how something works. An explanatory framework derived from an hypothesis which can be tested and confirmed or rejected.

Research use: a scientific statement which seeks to describe, explain and predict the nature of phenomena and their relationships. In science, theories normally start life as hypotheses which are repeatedly tested, gaining strength until they finally achieve the status of theories. A theoretical, or conceptual, framework provides a structure for establishing relationships between observations, or facts, in the advancement of knowledge. In this sense, theory and method are inextricably linked.

Example: gravitational theory: here Newton progressively refined his observations of the attraction between natural objects until he was able to express it in precise mathematical terms (*Mm/d2*; that is, the force of attraction between two bodies is given by the product of their masses divided by the square of the distance between them). For the practitioner working with sexual offenders theoretical explanations of sexually violent behaviour, from a number of disciplines, provide models of aetiology and intervention. Feminist theory, for example, directs attention at the role of negative representations of women in pornography and advertising as factors in masculine sex-role socialisation.

Related terms: hypothesis; observation; phenomenon.

Theory–practice gap

Everyday use: typically refers to the distance or potential conflict between theoretical accounts of the world and the lived experience of human beings.

Research use: this is a conceptual rather than a research issue; and has no direct application to the research process. However, as a dilemma it reminds us of the need to root research in the reality of those it involves. The term *praxis* denotes a linkage between theory and practice aimed at social change. Without such a link, practically based research runs the risk of generating theory for its own sake.

Example: in the discipline of psychiatry, much energy has been expended in constructing theoretical explanations and typologies of *psychopathy* by means of psychometric testing. Much less frequently, attention has been directed at the way such medical-legal categories are negotiated in the context of caring for patients with personality disorders. The former type of scholarly work offers little insight into the day-to-day difficulties involved in working with this challenging patient group.

Related term: theory.

Thesis

Everyday use: a set or series of linked theoretical statements.
Research use: usually refers to the final report produced by a research candidate studying for a higher degree by research. The written thesis (plus other materials if appropriate) is submitted in partial fulfilment of the academic requirements for the award of such a degree. The thesis then becomes the focus of discussion during the final *viva voce* (oral) examination.

Time-sampling

Everyday use: a systematic way of collecting representative examples of behaviour during structured observation.
Research use: allows researchers to manage data collection over a period of time without having to record the total event. Observations of behaviour, for example, might be divided into five-minute periods at intervals which are either fixed or random.
Example: a researcher may wish to explore the quality of verbal information during staff meetings. Time-sampling would permit segments of exchange to be observed and recorded rather than the total volume of interaction. Such segments will slowly build up the whole picture of the meetings.
Related terms: sampling; structured observation; time series.

Time series

Everyday use: a measurement of something at time intervals.
Research use: sets or series of measures of a single variable, which are recorded periodically at specific intervals and can present a global picture using an economic data collection technique.
Example: collecting 'smog' samples at certain times each day over a period of a year would contribute to an overall picture of 'smog' levels.
Related terms: time sampling; variable.

Trend

Everyday use: tendency to go in a particular direction.
Research use: a systematic increase or decrease in the observed values of a variable over a period of time.
Example: the amount of public spending is noted to increase

during a sale period.
Related term: time series.

Trial   *see **Double-Blind Trial/Experiment***

Triangulation

Everyday use: in nautical terms, 'getting a "fix"' on something. The analogy is drawn from the trigonometric process of navigation, where a location is often identified by plotting the point of intersection or third angle given by two known angles.
Research use: the practice of bringing another research method, or technique of data collection and analysis, to bear on a problem previously tackled by another method: for example, applying a quantitative design to the further analysis of a problem previously described qualitatively.
Example: in a research study on violent incidents occurring in a town centre, data could be collected from each of a number of sources: for example, incident reports; staff verbal reports; observational methods (cameras). Using data drawn from all these sources would constitute a triangulated study.
Related term: cross-validation.

Universe

Everyday use: all there is – generally applied to the physical universe.
Research use: all members of a population of interest.
Example: all midwives; of whom midwives working in England would form a sub-set from which a research sample might be drawn.
Related terms: population; sample; sampling frame.

Unstructured interview

Everyday use: a relaxed verbal exchange modelled on ordinary conversation.
Research use: an oral discussion involving two individuals, in which the researcher poses general questions without attempting to control the content or the direction of his/her informant's responses. This technique offers considerable flexibility by allowing informants to 'tell their stories' in the form of an unrestricted conversational narrative.
Example: interviews are characteristically unstructured. Within them informants are able to talk about basic issues, problems or perceptions regarding, for example, aspects of their care or life.
Related terms: focus group; focused interview; interview; verbal data.

Unstructured observation

Everyday use: looking at the way people behave in a variety of situations, in a free and unfocused manner.

Unstructured observation

Research use: a technique for collecting data about people and situations through direct, global observation which places no descriptive constraints on the researcher. His/her task is to give as complete a verbal description as possible of what is occurring, without categorising the material at this stage. This method gives the researcher an opportunity to assess the meaning of the situation for those involved. By contrast, *structured observation* techniques impose a clearly determined, coded protocol for the description of behaviour.

Example: by immersing him/herself in the daily life of a ward, the researcher may come to understand the culture, symbols, language and context of the environment being studied.

Related terms: ethnography; field observation; observation; participant observation.

Validity

Everyday use: legitimate; useful; suitable to perform a specific function.

Research use: the degree to which a research instrument or other data-gathering method measures what it is intended to measure. The greater the validity, the more likely is the study to help our understanding of the physical or social world, and to enable generalisation from its findings. *Face validity* is the immediate, apparent validity of the instrument. *Content validity* represents a more considered verdict on its content as judged by authorities in the field. Finally, *construct validity* is only achieved through a detailed critical analysis of the appropriateness with which relevant theoretical propositions are operationalised by the instrument. Internal validity is the extent to which the individual items which make up an instrument offer a coherent and logical description of what is being measured. External validity is the extent to which the test correlates with known valid measures of the same characteristic (i.e. its validity coefficient).

Examples: (1) the validity of measures of 'intelligence'. Do they actually measure abilities; or are they really a test of memory or of specific linguistic or numerical achievement? (2) The validity of 'personality' measures. Are there different types of personality corresponding to the various factorial methods (the *veridical* view); or are these simply convenient numerical techniques for describing relatively stable behaviours and attitudes (the *nominal* view)?

Related term: reliability.

'Value-free'

Everyday use: unaffected by personal values; considered in an objective way.

Research use: relates to the scientific quest to keep the personal values of the researcher out of the processes of data collection and interpretation. The classical empirical view is that this in turn will help the scientific community to obtain objective and neutral accounts of the world. There is, however, an alternative view that science is a value-laden enterprise; and that consequently genuinely neutral descriptions can never be achieved.

Example: 'value-free' descriptions are relatively easier to achieve within the experimental contexts of the natural sciences (though even here caution is required). However, for researchers studying social issues (e.g. rape or sexual violence), the approach needs to take account of constructional issues: that is, theoretical orientations; and the differing, socially constructed ideas and experiences of men and women.

Related term: objectivity.

Variable

Everyday use: something which is free to vary.

Research use: any characteristic, quality or attribute of an object or person which varies, and which can be observed and measured. An *independent variable* is one which can be varied by the researcher in order to observe its effects. By contrast, a *dependent variable* is one thought to vary in response to different levels of an independent variable, and therefore to be dependent upon it.

Example: in an experimental design specific variables can be controlled and manipulated to alter the relationship between them. For example, relative incidence of lung cancer is a dependent variable; and researchers have attempted to identify various causal independent variables – notably cigarette smoking.

Related terms: dependent variable; experimental design; independent variable.

Variance

Everyday use: the amount of variation occurring.

Research use: the variability occurring among scores in a

given data set. Variance provides a numerical way of describing the degree, or rate of change, occurring between units of data in a distribution. To describe a distribution adequately, there is a need for a measure of variance which expresses the extent to which scores differ from one another.

Example: two sets of scores achieved by the same individuals (say, scores on overt and covert aggression) are seen to have very similar mean scores. However, there is a much greater variance in one set of scores than in the other. This tells us that these variables are displaying differential effects in the same sample; and that therefore there is a subtle difference between them requiring further investigation.

Related terms: data; distribution; mean; range; standard deviation.

Verbal data

Everyday use: data consisting of words.

Research use: data collected in written or oral form, generally by means of a questioning technique such as an interview or questionnaire. Verbal data may also be obtained from archival materials, personal documents such as journals or diaries, recorded interviews and in written protocols requested from respondents. Verbal data may offer insights into underlying attitudes and values, organisational patterns and professional trends.

Example: various forms of verbal data are collected during an exploratory study of the manner in which receptionists talk to their customers in different settings: for example, in factories, surgeries and offices.

Related terms: discourse analysis; ethnography; qualitative data.

Verification

Everyday use: to verify something is to make efforts to determine whether or not it is true.

Research use: research methods are designed to *verify* the propositions which lie at the heart of the research question. In order to achieve this, a variety of qualitative and quantitative methods are used. The term *verification* came to have a special meaning for a group of philosophers known as the *logical positivists*, who advanced the influential theory that, in order to be meaningful, a proposition must be verified by recourse either to mathematical logic or to empirical evidence derived from the natural sciences. This is known as the *verification principle* or as the *principle of verifiability*. This principle was later challenged by the philosopher Karl Popper, who put forward in its place the *theory of falsifiability*. This introduces the notion that, in order to be meaningful, a proposition must satisfy the condition that there exists a possible method of showing it to be false.

Example: methods of verification will differ according to the type(s) of data which are being analysed. For example, behaviourist approaches to therapy rely upon behavioural frequencies; psychoanalytic approaches invest in the patient's gaining improved insight into the deeply rooted causes of his/her problem; and pharmacological studies examine behavioural and psychological responses to varying drug doses.

Related terms: qualitative method; quantitative methods.

Vertical study   *see **Longitudinal study***

Vignette

Everyday use: a vignette is a painting or photograph in which attention is concentrated on the central details, with other areas excluded by an opaque oval or round border.

Research use: the notion of a vignette is applied by analogy to discussion of a real-life situation. A brief, fictitious or factual description of an event, to which respondents are asked to react. Comments on, or ratings of vignettes can elicit information about the respondent's knowledge, perceptions or opinions regarding the phenomenon under study.

Example: a vignette of a typical incident in psychiatric care can be used to provide an indirect measure of nurses' attitudes, stereotypes and habitual ways of thinking about mental illnesses or personality disorders.

Related term: self-report techniques.

Vulnerable subject

Everyday use: to be 'vulnerable' is to be at special risk of exploitation or attack.

Research use: a vulnerable subject is either (1) an individual who is easily accessible to researchers and thus at risk of being over-researched; or (2) an individual who is not able to assess meaningfully the implications or risks of taking part in a proposed study.

Example: it is difficult for members of captive groups (e.g. prisoners) to give genuinely voluntary consent regarding participation in drug trials.

Related terms: ethics; informed consent.

~ W/ X / Y / Z ~

Weighting

Everyday use: giving more importance or prominence to some aspects rather than others.

Research use: weighting is a disproportional sampling frame, sometimes used in groups which are greatly different in size. Here more members are recruited from the smaller groups than would be indicated by strict proportional sampling, to allow for a better estimate of overall values.

Example: in order to obtain adequate representation of ethnic minorities in a student nurse population, the researcher may 'oversample' (increase the numbers) for these sub-samples.

Related terms: random-stratified sample; sample.

X–Y axes

Everyday use: an axis is a pivotal point or important 'coming together'.

Research use: conventionally a graph has two axes at right angles to each other: the *x-axis* (the positive part of the horizontal axis or *x-coordinate*) moves across the page to the right; and the *y-axis* (the positive part of the vertical axis or *y-coordinate*) moves up the page. The two axes bisect each other at right angles. The system is named after the philosopher and mathematician Rene Descartes (1596–1650) who invented it. It is extremely useful and universally known; and forms the basis of a large proportion of graphic illustration carried out in research of all kinds. Horizontal (x) and vertical (y) axes are typically used to plot the relationship between two variables.

Example: see for example the graphs presented under *bar chart*; *line graph*; *scattergram*; and *skewness*. Note that the vertical (*y*) axis is not always drawn where clarity does not demand it; but it is notionally there!

Related terms: see examples given above.

Z-score

Everyday use: in statistics, a score which is standardised on the normal distribution. Also known as a *standard score*.

Research use: it is sometimes difficult to compare scores obtained on one measure with scores obtained on another (for example, achievement tests in English with similar tests in mathematics). The task becomes much simpler if both sets of scores are standardised in terms of the normal curve. This is done by working out a standard score (*z-score*) for individuals on both variables and comparing the two. The z-score for an individual is worked out using the following equation:

$$z = [x - M] / \sigma$$

where *x* is the individual score; *M* is the mean score for that sample; and σ is the sample standard deviation. The standard score can also be used to work out the probability under the normal curve of obtaining such a result.

Example: in a public health survey, a large number of men had their heights measured. These were found to be normally distributed with a mean of 172.5 cm and a standard deviation of 6.25 cm. What proportion of men in this sample would have a height of 180 cm or more? From the above equation, the z-score of a man with a height of 180 cm is ([180–172.5] / 6.25) = 1.20. Looking at a table of probabilities under the normal curve, we find that the probability of obtaining such a result is 0.115. This figure is also the proportion of cases in the sample likely to have a height of 180 cm or more.

Related terms: mean; normal distribution; standard deviation; standard score; survey.